Normativity Within the Bounds of Plural Reasons

THE APPLIED ETHICS REVOLUTION

SERGIO CREMASCHI

Normativity Within the Bounds
of Plural Reasons

THE APPLIED ETHICS REVOLUTION

NSU SUMMERTALK VOL. 1 | 2007

An NSU Series Edited by:

DAG PETERSSON
ASGER SØRENSEN

NSU Press

Published in Sweden by NSU Press
Kungsgatan 32
SE-75321 Uppsala SWEDEN
http://www.nsuweb.net

Produced by Söderströms Förlag
Georgsgatan 29A, 2 vån
PO Box 870
FI-00101 Helsingfors, FINLAND
http://www.soderstrom.fi

Printed by Nord Print Ab
Helsingfors, 2007

Distributed by Århus University Press
Langelandsgade 177
8200 Århus N DENMARK
http://www.unipress.dk

ISBN 978-87-87564-07-6

Contents

Acknowledgements

No book is exclusively a result of the author's efforts. This is even more true of this one, since it is very short and the result of little exertion by the writer. The main thrust was given by Asger Sørensen, who proposed my invitation as a lecturer at the Nordic Summer University 2006 Summer Session at Kääriku, Estonia, besides warmly encouraging the transformation of my two lectures into three, and the three lectures into a short book, as well as suggesting a number of conclusions to my argument that I had not fully spelled out. My thanks go also to all the participants, who were kind enough to listen patiently to my lectures and to discuss what I had to say most stimulatingly. Other people have tried hard to force me into making the hazy conjectures scattered about in my history of twentieth century ethics[1] somewhat less vague: the first is Giovanni De Grandis, whose lengthy review-essay[2] provided me with a list of topics and even the title for the present essay; after him, my friends and colleagues Massimo Reichlin, Roberta Sala, Roberto Mordacci, and Sara Casati from whom I have learned anything I may happen to know about bioethics; and my students Matteo Miglio, Letizia Abrate, Elena Pavesi, Alessandra Provera, Elisa Buccaresi from whose dissertations I have learned what was left to learn on applied ethics at large, and then Javier Muguerza (a non-believer in applied ethics and a couple of other things as well) the conversations with whom have left some traces on this essay.

Finally, I have to thank Daphne Hughes who revised the language, and Dag Petersson who took care of the publication.

[1] Sergio Cremaschi, *L'etica del Novecento. Dopo Nietzsche* (Rome: Carocci, 2005).

[2] Giovanni De Grandis, "The Rise (and Fall ?) of Normative Ethics. A Critical Notice of Sergio Cremaschi's L'etica del Novecento," in *Etica e Politica /Ethics & Politics*, 7/1 (2006), 1–11. http://www.units.it/etica/2006_1/DEGRANDIS.htm).

PREFACE

'I am afraid if you want a guide to behaviour you'll be disappointed... No philosopher ever did produce a guide to behaviour, even when he thought that that was what he was doing... The thing is just a meditation on a few concepts.'

'The relation of love to truth and justice and some small matters of that sort, I gather.'

'Some small matters of that sort! But the application must remain for the individual to decide.'

'Poor individual. No one ever really looks after him. Now what I want is a sort of case book of morals like a guide to etiquette...'

'Ordinary people can't apply philosophy anyway. I doubt if even philosophers can.'

'People can use moral concepts, as you used the concept of truth just to persuade me. Anyone can do this.'

'Maybe. But I think moral philosophy is something hopelessly personal. It just can't be communicated.'

Iris Murdoch, *A Fairly Honourable Defeat* (London: Penguin 1970), 46–47.

In chapter one I will try to reconstruct a plot, or a hidden agenda, in the discussion in ethics between the beginning of the twentieth century and 1958, the year of a decisive turning point in ethics, both Anglo-Saxon and Continental, and strangely enough also the year of the beginning of the end of the Cold War, of post-Tridentine Catholicism, and perhaps something else. My hypothesis will be that there are two similar starting points for the Anglo-Saxon and the Continental twentieth-century discussion, the philosophies of Henry Sidgwick and Friedrich Nietzsche, both expressions of some kind of ethical scepticism, and that a third, somewhat analogous starting-point could be found in Émile Durkheim, the proponent of the unrealisable dream of the *morale laïque*. I will discuss how far the diagnosis formulated by Karl-Otto Apel of a kind of 'parallel convergence'[1] between existentialism and analytic philosophy, based on the shared division of facts and values that eventually justified two kinds of 'decisionism' is useful in making sense of the agenda of the discussion.

In the second chapter I will discuss the reasons for two parallel U-turns around 1958 which brought back traditional schools of normative ethics, 'deontologism' and utilitarianism, as well as the reasons for criticism to both schools from the heterogeneous alignment of virtue ethics.

In the third chapter I will discuss the remarkable phenomenon of the emergence, starting with the sixties or the early seventies, of 'applied' ethics. I examine the reasons, both theoretical and political, for the revival, the point to which applied ethics may look as a grand return of a casuistic and natural law way of thinking, or in Alan Donagan's words a case of "reverse subversion" of the modern secular world by traditional Scholastic ways of thinking, and the difficult coexistence between general normative ethics and procedures for settling issues in a 'reasonable' way while dissent on issues of principle is as alive as ever. Then I try to draw a provisional moral. My suggestions are that (i) casuistry is more alive than ever; (ii) natural law thinking is more alive than ever; (iii) moral dilemmas never arise; (iv) moral dissent is treatable, with the right strategy; (v) practical philosophy does not need the same degree of exactness as the theoretical sciences but this is no obstacle to its working in practice.

---

[1] This non-euclidean or baroque geometrical formula is not Apel's, but is taken from the Italian politician Aldo Moro.

CHAPTER I

From the Death of Ethics to the Normative Turn

Twentieth Century Ethics After the Death of Ethics

The discussion reconstructed in this essay had its start at the turn of the nineteenth century, after Nietzsche and Sidgwick proposed two versions, the Anglo-Saxon and the Continental, of moral scepticism, and Durkheim tried unsuccessfully to deliver the Arabian Phoenix of the Secular Morality, and then followed two rather tortuous but parallel paths. These two parallel paths led from the 'normative scepticism' ruling in the first decades of the twentieth century to the 'normative turn' of 1958. The normative scepticism prevailing in the first half of the century was a quite heterogenous phenomenon, consisting of the prevailing of currents that tended to deny the possibility of normative ethics as such on both sides of the Channel. The prevailing Anglo-Saxon currents tended to restrict the task of ethics to that of a philosophy *of* morality; the Continental currents tended to substitute ethics with 'analytics of existence,' that is, with a phenomenological description of the world as a place where we are both damned to choose and left without criteria for choosing.

The normative turn took place around 1958 thanks to the contribution of several thinkers, in the English-speaking world Philippa Foot, Peter Geach, Elisabeth Anscombe, Kurt Baier, and in Germany Hans-Georg Gadamer. The ensuing story has been one of controversies between two (or three) kinds of normative ethics, namely neo-Utilitarian, Kantian, and Virtue Ethics. The controversies have carried surprising processes of self-transformation and convergence, till at a certain point they have been accompanied, or superseded, by the applied ethics revolution. The latter has carried the most decisive refutation of ethical scepticism, similar to the refutation of the Parmenidean paradox that was staged *deambulando*, or just by walking. The decisive argument was the discovery of new methods of moral reasoning ethics, the first of which was Beauchamp and Childress's principlism, that make moral dissent on ultimate principle compatible with convergence on intermediate principles.[1]

Three Diagnoses of Death for Ethics

Let us take a step back. Towards the end the nineteenth century in the three main linguistic areas in Europe three leading thinkers formulated a diagnosis of what could be labelled, in some way or another, the death of ethics.

Henry Sidgwick, the son of an Anglican Rector (born 1838, died 1900, thirteen days after Nietzsche), with his *Methods of Ethics* of 1874 established a kind of canon that still rules in disguise in Anglo-Saxon ethics. While trying to defend John Stuart Mill's version of a utilitarian ethics as a viable 'new' morality, exempt from the inconsistencies of traditional authoritarian morality, against the attacks waged by the intuitionist William Whewell, he resorted to a memorable kind of waste land strategy, by proving that little could be proved in ethics and accordingly, even if we admit that utilitarianism does not hold, at least intuitionism (supposedly, traditional morality in philosophical togs) fares much worse, and accordingly utilitarian ways of reasoning should be adopted *faute de mieux* at least by the educated elite, while the uneducated mass may be left to traditional morality, since this is a cheaper way to approximately the same prescriptions.

More in detail, rules of the 'old morality,' such as not lying, keeping promises, being just, are – apart from lacking a true justification – impracticable, since they are not enforceable in any precise sense and leave marginal cases about which they have nothing to say;

a) on the contrary, the basic rule of the 'new morality' – benevolence – is plausible and it is to this very rule that common-sense morality tends to have recourse in order to solve untreatable cases of perplexity or conflict between two rules of the old morality, but

b) benevolence cannot be enforced in a precise sense in all cases, because of limits in acquiring and processing information carrying uncertainty on consequences of lines of action and, accordingly on what our duty is;

c) besides, it is as well not to teach the new morality to the majority of agents because of its negative side-effects on moral motivation that is kept more alive by a kind of dogmatic belief in a sacred character of moral rules; so the overall result would be better (in terms of benevolence) in case the mass go on practising a second best for the new morality, that is the traditional common-sense morality, and the elite be left free to allow for exceptions to traditional rules without letting the mass know;

d) finally, benevolence may be adopted as a rule albeit its applications are no more definite, in principle, than those of the rules of traditional morality and its justification is no more plausible than that of the opposite rule – rational egoism; so elite humanitarianism is just an option, it is practicable with a high degree of uncertainty, and needs be kept secret from the mass;

e) if we could know that there were a moral governance of the world, implying that God existed, there would be a reason to adopt the new morality of benevolence, since we would have a reason in favour of benevolence against egoism; but since we cannot know that God exists, we are left with an unjustified option between benevolence and egoism.[2]

Friedrich Nietzsche, the son of a Lutheran Pastor (born 1844, died 1903), in a number of brilliant essays and literary works spread the word of the death of God and the coming of what I propose be translated as *ultra-man*. His message, though understood at first in a cheap version, as an expression of fin-de-siècle decadentism, and then in either a criminal version by racists and anti-Semites or in a distorted version by the existentialists, had a powerful impact and is still taken seriously, indeed with a number of good reasons, since what he says is deeper than what Sidgwick has to say. Nietzsche's lesson is:

a) Good and Evil are adjectives insensibly transformed into substantives; originally only 'good' and 'bad' as descriptions of social conditions existed, and they used to denote members of the upper and of the lower class;

15

b) Kant was wrong because duty, conscience, virtue are modified forms of our basic drives, which in turn are beyond egoism and altruism, and are just one more metamorphosis of such basic drives;

c) Bentham was wrong no less than Kant, because benevolence too is a condensed form of our basic drives, and as such it is no more altruistic than selfishness and greed;

d) there is no real room for a norm-yielding morality since the 'authentic' attitude lies beyond the distinction between the description and prescription, the true fulfilment of the Christian virtue of truthfulness consists in 'becoming what we already are' or in living fully our "will to power."[3]

Émile Durkheim, the son of a Rabbi, who was born in 1858 and died in 1917, founded a new discipline – sociology – as a side-effect to his quest for a new scientific morality. His book on morality, that in his view was to be the summary of his life's work, was left unfinished and soon forgotten by both sociologists, who found it a non-sociological work, and philosophers, who disregarded it as a work by a non-philosopher.

Durkheim's claims, in the published works and in the fragments of his intended book, were:

a) a process of secularisation has excluded duties to God from morality, reducing it to duties to fellow-human beings;

b) the risk of such a process is "anomy," a condition where growing masses of individuals are left without any internalised steering device as a result of the lessening of the motivating force of moral rules no longer felt as holy in their origins;

c) discipline is required as a means to happiness, since the individual left facing too many choices is overwhelmed by anxiety;

d) discipline is required as a means to coordination, since an internalised adhesion to the group's needs is the only way of avoiding the costs and negative side-effects of coercion on a massive scale;

e) attachment to society is required as a source of motivation for individuals who need to be motivated by an object of love, and a transcendent object of this kind has always been provided by society, even if under the disguise of God;

f) Bentham was wrong because his idea of utility of coincidence between collective and individual interest is too simple, being unable to account for those cases where the individual's interest does *not* converge with the collective interest;

g) Kant was wrong because his absolute autonomy is impossible and his unique imperative ineffective;

h) secularisation aims at autonomy; this is made possible in general by science that provides man with the means of controlling the external milieu instead of being controlled by the latter; in the domain of morality science does not provide any means for control, but yields knowledge of necessity thus ending with the (slightly disappointing) conclusion that we may become autonomous in so far as we surrender to necessity.[4]

...and One Prognosis of Resurrection With Transfiguration

After the mourning of the death of God by three such illustrious sons of religious ministers, one is tempted to wish one had been born in a congregation where ministers don't marry or, better, there are no ministers. Such was the case with John Dewey, born a Congregationalist in 1859, died in 1952, having lost his religious beliefs no less than the first three authors, though having kept the sort of preacher's attitude that is unavoidably universalised in congregations where there are no appointed preachers, and which is the less appealing trait of his contribution. Yet, Dewey's message was at least not mournful and far from implying any farewell to normative ethics. Deweys' claims were:

a) Platonism was wrong because there is *not* one substantive, self-standing and unchanging human nature, since the latter results from interaction between a living organism and its natural/social milieu;

b) Bentham was wrong because he never questioned the existence of *one* pre-established end for human action, but limited himself instead

17

to questioning current ideas on the nature of such an end and identified such nature with pleasure;

c) Kant was wrong in so far as he, no less than Bentham, adopted the assumption that desires arise from quest for pleasure; he was right in so far as it is true that good is found in activity, will itself is the end, satisfaction of given desires is to be differed and subordinated to an overarching law;

d) ethical 'naturalism' is in a sense the right view, since morality has no distinct *ethical* goal, and it is not ruled by distinct *ethical* procedures; ethics is just one part among others of a set of tools aimed at carrying out a wider task, the task of bringing about fully blossoming and satisfactory human life.[5]

To sum up, Dewey was drawing a diagnosis on the status of modern moral philosophy and the sources of its malaise rather similar to those of Sidgwick, Nietzsche, and Durkheim, and in particular he was attacking both Kant and Bentham for the same reasons (the reasons that have been circulating in the last 25 years as the astonishing discovery of Alisdair MacIntyre and Bernard Williams) but with none of Nietzsche's politically incorrect implications, no flavour of Sidgwick's perplexing elitist esoteric morality, and no concession to Durkheim's authoritarian democracy. Dewey still believed in rationally justified, albeit not 'founded,' normative ethics together with human equality, human rights, radical democracy, and even universalism.

Now the question is, how did it happen that between 1903 and 1958 the received view on both sides of the Channel, and of the Atlantic, was that, given recent theoretical developments that had proven any *foundation* of ethics to have been irremediably shaken, normative ethics was to be declared unfortunately impossible, with all obvious implications for human equality, human rights, democracy, and universalism? As argued by Richard Bernstein, after the Kuhnian turn in the philosophy of science, pragmatist themes have unavoidably come back on the agenda, and an old ideas, pragmatist anti-foundationalism, has unavoidably become the *dernier cri* albeit formulated in new words.[6] The point is that lack of foundation, triumphantly or sadly announced, has never been tantamount to impossibility of justification.

The Anti-normative Turn: The Anglo-Saxon Version

In the Anglo-Saxon world after 1903, the year Moore's *Principles* were published, the discussion concentrated on metaethics, leaving normative ethics aside, basically as a field about which philosophers had nothing special to add, apart from some kind of logical hygiene, or as a field where conclusive proofs for rationally deciding for one line of conduct were not available, and accordingly philosophers could help with preliminaries but could not deal with the thing in itself. This is why in the following decade we find various kinds of non-cognitivism dominating, with a cognitivism school of thought left, neo-intuitionism, but fighting rather on defence, since Sidgwick's main claim on the unavoidable conflict of moral rules in every concrete individual case was going unquestioned and accordingly cognitivism was good for theory but not for practice.

What made non-cognitivism a winner in the academic dispute was the circumstance that it was a philosophical expression of a widespread state of mind. the unquestioned assumption was the fact-value dichotomy, a claim that expressed in a more sober, British wording the tragic Weberian view of *Entzäuberung* (stripping the world of its magic).

This assumption, as most basic assumptions was never clearly articulated (all the praise so-called analytic philosophers bestow on clear articulation of concepts) because it proved so convincing without a clear articulation that it was made to rest on two or three semi-processed arguments, from time to time confused one with another. The first, and most drastic justification was Hume's guillotine, taken from Hume's conclusion in the Enquiries according to which statements that make sense include only statements of matters of fact or analytic statements and all the rest is simply meaningless.[7] This was the master-argument for the Neo-positivists. According to Hans Reichenbach an intellectualistic and aprioristic ethics of the Kantian kind is impossible, because *a priori* synthetic judgements cannot be legitimately formulated, and accordingly normative ethics as such is a contradiction in terms.

> The axioms of geometry can be made true statements when they are regarded as physical statements... The axioms of ethics, in contrast, cannot be made cognitive statements at all; there is no interpretation in which they can be called true. They are volitional decisions.[8]

Commands are something different from assertions; what kind of authority a moral command has is far from clear; but it is clear enough that it cannot derive its own authority from rational reasons, for "a scientific philosophy cannot supply moral guidance."[9]

The second argument was the naturalistic fallacy, Moore's over-emphasized argument out of which – according to the *vulgata* – analytic ethics as such was born. In 1922 Moore himself admitted he had advanced a blurred argument that points to more than one kind of fallacy, the *co-extensivists fallacy*, that is a confusion between co-extension and identity, with the unjustified claim of being able to analyse all moral concepts in a reductionist way, and the *naturalistic-and-metaphysical* fallacy, that is the unwarranted claim that moral concepts denote properties, either natural or metaphysical.[10] The main remarks worth making are that, as far as the first sense of the fallacy is concerned, the requirements for definition accepted are extremely demanding, and most definitions are much more loose, as Moore himself clearly stated in his later contributions to philosophy of language. As far as the second sense of the fallacy is concerned, it was meant to play against hedonism, in favour of a definition of the good that be "non natural," but it circulated instead for several decades under the cloak of the alleged master-argument for non-cognitivism.

The third argument was Hume's law, sometimes believed to be more or less the same argument as the naturalistic fallacy, while in fact it was a quite distinct, albeit parallel argument. As Prior aptly distinguished, it supports a kind of 'syntactical non-naturalism,' while Moore's argument supports semantical non-naturalism (and by the way, both fail to support a more demanding claim, an 'ontological' non-naturalism, that is what most analytic philosophers used to believe they had actually proved).[11] Hume's law is an absolutely undeniable argument, but may be used in two opposite directions. By Henri Poincaré it was used in 1912 in order to stress inherent limits of science, proving that science could be left alone, since it need not meddle with religion, metaphysics, and ethics.[12] Karl Popper in 1947 used it in order to stress the limits of ethics, proving that, since no ethical truth could ever be proved, normative issues should be left to private decisions and public agreements of the members of an open society.[13] A famous argument published by Searle in 1966 aimed at refuting Hume's law met with the success it deserved, since Hume's law in fact proved none of the consequences Popper believed it could prove, but also bestowed on its author undeserved fame in so far as it was already in David Ross and Richard Price, albeit not meant to refute Hume's law.[14]

A widespread impression is that normative ethics in the first half of the twentieth century simply disappeared.[15] There is a grain of truth in such a view, but in fact in both the Anglo-Saxon and the German-speaking world there were two parallel, and mutually unknown, trends of normative ethics that fought back the rising trends of non-cognitivism and existentialism with little success, due primarily to their too modest claims. The two alternatives in the Anglo-Saxon world were cognitivism, in the shape of neo-intuitionism, and non-cognitivism, in the shape of emotivism or prescriptivism. In the course of the discussion the latter was the winner, and in the fifties it seemed to be *the* normative ethics of analytic philosophy *tout court*. The neo-intuitionist ethics formulated by David Ross and Richard Prichard as a result of their criticism of George Moore's bizarre non-hedonistic utilitarianism was objectivist; non-naturalistic, anti-sceptical in metaethics, and ironically anti-sceptical in theory and sceptical in practice in matters of normative ethics. The conundrum lied in the discovery of the existence of a plurality of sources of moral obligation on the one hand immunized by the claim that, facing the individual case, we have no final criterion for ordering different kinds of obligations, and are left with a list of possible reasons for acting and no criterion, apart from an invocation to 'judgement' (half-Aristotelian and half-Kantian).

As Alan Donagan acutely remarked, the poison was already there in Sidgwick, and it poisoned both Moore's consequentialist version and Ross's and Prichard's pluralist-deontological version of neo-intuitionism. Sidgwick's lesson was: a) the empirical element in ethics is far from decisive, since pleasure and happiness are elusive notions; b) the *a priori* element cannot be dispensed with, and there are indeed (a few) a priori ethical truths; c) such truths are in a conflictive relationship with one another (no hierarchical ordering); d) and as a consequence there is no definite duty that can be known as such.

The fatal point was Sidgwick's admission that Bentham was right in his criticism of intuitionism on point (d) and thus no ethical theory whatsoever may provide real guidance to conduct. It is not by chance that Sidgwick's *Methods of Ethics* in their first edition ended with the two words "inevitable failure."[16]

Moore, Ross, and Prichard forgot the two final words and went on trying to build various versions of a non-utilitarian ethical system on the basis of his conclusion. Moore's version dropped the hedonistic element of utilitarianism while keeping the rest. Thus it consisted of: a) utilitarianism as a moral ontology (primacy of the good over the right); b) intuitionism as a moral epistemology (knowledge of the good a priori); c) a limited scepticism, not theoretical but practical (common-sense morality rules are most of the time good approximations to the result of a calculus; in dubious cases the latter is strictly impossible; a good approximation is: consider consequences limited in time and in space). Moore's practical lesson, according to Donagan, was: conform to conventional morality when no major doubt arises; in case of novel or dubious situations, go against conventional morality whenever you feel like doing so; in such cases, *faute de mieux*, adopt an urbane kind of egoism as a working criterion, or take account of yourself and your friends.

Ross's version was alternative to Moore's: it discarded the hedonistic element as well, but it reduced the consequentialist way of reasoning to one particular case among others. Ross's version consisted in the sum of the following claims: a) there are intuitions of several kinds and they are there just because they are there (one has to keep a promise because one has made it); b) but all cases are over-determined and there is always a conflict of obligations; c) in order to select 'real' obligations one has to perceive the case as a whole by *aisthesis* in terms of unity/harmony/ balance in the overall situation. Ross's theoretical lesson is that there is knowledge of duties, and it is so obvious that only by a sophism could one contend that there is no duty to keep a promise when one has made it. Ross's practical lesson, again according to Donagan is: a) in every case you never face a clear-cut duty; b) in every dubious case you always have considerations for justifying any alternative course of action; c) in such cases, adopt a mild kind of 'I feel like doing x' attitude as a working criterion.

The alternative basic theoretical solution was non-cognitivism – a kind of outright subjectivism, or scepticism both in theory and in practice. The first wave of non-cognitivism was emotivism, which appeared in a rudimentary shape first in the Scandinavian and German-speaking countries in the teens and twenties of the twentieth century and reached England, and then the United States, mainly through German intellectual emigration in the thirties. Bertrand Russell, Julius Ayer, Charles Stevenson, the best known proponents of the view, agreed on one basic outlook, that is, the claim that science and values (morality, politics, law) are separated. The would-be theoretical justification of such an outlook rested on a fragile basis, the idea of emotive meaning as opposed to descriptive meaning, an idea that was found in Ogden and Richards's *The Meaning of Meaning*,[17] and that melted away as developments in linguistic theory and the birth of pragmatics out of the Oxford philosophy of language outlined the existence of a plurality of uses of language, besides description and expression of states of mind.

The other version of non-cognitivism was prescriptivism, as worked out by Richard Hare shortly after Karl Popper launched Hume's law.[18] The novelty of this approach is the fact of doing away with the muddled notion of emotive meaning. The continuity with the former version was provided by the claim that there is a logical division between statements of fact and valuations and thus there is also an absolute argumentative division between science and ethics.

Let me note that for a long time, up to the seventies, the image of analytic ethics available to Continental philosophers was an odd one, that of a technocratic and scientist worldview that left no room for ethics. It was based on Russell and Ayer. Cognitivist authors like Ross and Prichard were unknown and incomprehensible and they could not fit in the received image of analytic ethics, since neo-intuitionism, or what was left of intuitionism, albeit eventually inconclusive and sceptical in practice, was not empiricist, relativist, and subjectivist, as Continental philosophers expected analytic ethics to be. This is still reflected in a passage of one of the most famous of Apel's essays. He writes:

> The intertwining of mysticism and existential subjectivism or 'transcendental solipsism' in Wittgensteins's considerations on ethics corresponds to a typical problem in modern Existentialism… how can theoretical philosophy in general say anything, with a claim to its inter-subjective validity, about what is by definition subjective and individual. A special aspect of this problem emerges now also within the context of analytic metaethics. In fact the question is asked within this context: whence does a metaethics, which is descriptive and objective, with a self-image as a value-free science, take criteria for singling out morally relevant language uses, which cannot in any way be won from the grammatical structure of language as it can be objectively described.[19]

As Apel was almost right in pointing out, there was also a German version of the anti-normative turn. This was existentialism, but also this Continental form of ethical scepticism had to fight, no less than non-cognitism, against a cognitivist opponent, in this case the philosophy of values. This opponent too was soon defeated and for similar reasons, namely deploying too weak an armament.

Let me recall first what the claims of phenomenology and the philosophy of values were.

Values had been introduced by nineteenth-century neo-Kantians as an alternative to Kant's 'maxims.' Values were supposed to play a role in epistemology, aesthetics, and ethics, and this is probably the main reason why – given the primacy of art and the historico-cultural disciplines after Romanticism – to late nineteenth-century thinkers they seemed more appealing than maxims.

In the beginning of the twentieth-century, after Husserl's formulation of a program for phenomenology as an anti-psychologistic and anti-empiricist alternative to positivism and philosophies of life, 'values' looked like something non-empirical and non-psychological enough as to provide the foundation for the a-priori ethics the phenomenological movement was, given its assumptions, almost forced to formulate. Max Scheler was later overemphasized – either to be cherished or to be abhorred – as the proponent of phenomenological ethics. The weaknesses of this approach, based on 'material' intuition of various kinds of values and thus on justification of duties on the basis of an intuition of the primacy of one value or another, are well known and have played their part in discrediting the phenomenological movement as such. But there was also another comparatively forgotten version of the phenomenological approach to normative ethics, Adolf Reinach's theory of 'acts.' According to this theory the source of obligation is not in a human 'nature,' understood in a physical or quasi-physical sense, for grounding or justifying universal rights or universal duties, but instead in 'acts' of conscience, such as promising, communicating etc. that are performed in an inter-subjective framework; ability by any subject to perform such acts is enough to include her or him in a community tied together by mutual obligations.[20]

Reiner's approach was forgotten, perhaps with the exception of

Edith Stein, and superseded by Scheler's and Hartman's solipsistic and contemplative approach to values that leaves the transition from metaethics to normative ethics, or the grounding of obligation in a mist, analogous to but thicker than, the uncertainties of Ross's *prima facie* duties. The most convincing version of the phenomenological route from values to a would-be normative ethics was described by Nicolai Hartman (even if he always refused to define himself as a phenomenologist) in the following way: a) values belonging to different spheres of ideal existence are out there, waiting to be 'known' through intuition (i.e., non-empirical knowledge of being, not of phenomena, or states of consciousness); b) thus ethics is one chapter of ontology; c) values are the laws to which every being conforms itself not in so far as it is but instead in so far as it ought to be. Before the question "What ought I to do?" come s a more general question: "What is there in life, or better in the world, that is valuable?"; d) Values do exist, like mathematical entities (note that this is different from Scheler's claim that values do not exist, but limit themselves to be valid; e) as a consequence, no normative relativism of a Nietzschian kind may be condoned; f) but, as a side-effect, values are also independent of the 'goods,' that is, the things that have value; g) since all values, including those of vitality and utility, have an ideal reality, some hierarchy has to be introduced among values, and this hierarchy too is known intuitively; h) the role of philosophical ethics is that of a protrepticon to an ethical life; an educated individual would develop an ability to 'discern' values in real existence; this is all that philosophy can do for an ethical life.[21]

The comment is in order that this is not very much, and did not help Hartman in his real life between 1933 and 1945, that of one out of many loyal University Professors under the Nazi regime.

Existentialism was the winner in the Continental dispute over values and by the fifties phenomenology and the philosophy of values were surviving in a few niches. The main claims of Existentialism were the following: a) no general rule is available; each individual situation is unique; b) values are not discovered but 'enacted' (existence comes before essence). This does not sound like a formidable set of theoretical arguments, and in fact existentialism owed its own success to the circumstance of expressing well a widespread mood, not to the strength of its arguments. It was first of all a cultural phenomenon from the teens, the years when Franz Rosenzweig wrote the *Star of Redemption* while Wittgenstein was writing the *Tractatus*; a phenomenon primarily theological, and only secondly philosophical; a phenomenon consisting in a double negation, the refusal of liberal theology, which was the refusal of the old theology as an undue mix of metaphysics and biblical exegesis; the double refusal amounted to vindicating the autonomy of faith from ethics, after the liberal vindication of the autonomy of ethics from religion; the phenomenon consisted also in a return to the kind of problems that had been central for the seventeenth century at the time of casuistical probabilism and Jansenist refusal of casuistry, that is conscience, uncertainty, decision, subjectivity; the phenomenon of 'classical' existentialism (Martin Heidegger and Jean-Paul Sartre) consisted in repeating what theological existentialism had to say making it comprehensible – at least to a point, the incomprehensible residue added more popularity – for the lay/secular public.

The apparent triumph of the existentialist cum non-cognitivist odd alignment in the forties and fifties made an old sceptical claim look like the new wisdom for a disenchanted modern world: *De valoribus non est disputandum*. This is illustrated well by two famous arguments from both camps. Sartre told the story of a former student who had asked for his advice – whether he should look after his mother who had been left a widow or join De Gaulle's army in England. Sartre refused, giving this memorable answer: you are free; choose, and be the man you will have chosen to be.[22] If this sounds disappointing it may be enough to look again at Popper's famous argument for the open society: there is no ethical truth; values are decisions; thus the only rule that I may give is to respect different coexisting decisions.[23] This being the state of the art, MacIntyre's reconstruction of the state of moral argument in the modern world was not so implausible, either. According to MacIntyre, there are three characteristics of contemporary moral debates: a) "The conceptual incommensurability of the rival arguments";[24] b) the fact that they nonetheless "purport to be *impersonal* rational arguments";[25] c) a resulting 'moral pluralism' as an "an unharmonious melange of ill-assorted fragments."[26] Is this the last word to say on ethics in contemporary society? I believe it is not.

A few intermediate conclusions may be the following:

a) a parallel between existentialism and non-cognitivism has been formulated several times by several commentators; this parallel sounded astonishing only because of a story of mutual hatred between Continental and Anglo-Saxon philosophers, based on mutual simplified images of arrogant technocracy vs. self-indulging obscurity;[27]

b) a parallel between new intuitionism and the philosophy of values has never been drawn primarily because of mutual ignorance; instead, there was, so to say, a Continental Intuitionism (Hartman) and an Anglo-Saxon philosophy of values (Ross); this contradicts Apel's account, since there were in both areas trends that were cognitivist (at least in principle), and yet, both were sceptical in practice: values or duties do have objective validity, but in individual situations everything is left to individual decision unaided by theory;

c) and yet, in the Anglo-Saxon world in the eighties and nineties some existentialist themes emerged in a new key, with no connection with non-cognitivism or emotivism, but instead within the framework of new trends, new sentimentalism, expressivism, anti-theory; and most of all in Iris Murdoch's own combination of Wittgensteinian philosophy, Existentialism, and Neoplatonism. In Murdoch's words, both existentialism and the Wittgensteinian philosophy are a "vulgar" version of the true doctrine, which is Platonism, and

Good is the distant source of light, it is the unimaginable object of our desire. Our fallen nature knows only its name and its perfection. That is the idea which is vulgarised by existentialists and linguistic philosophers when they make it into a mere matter of personal choice. It cannot be defined, not because it is a function of our freedom, but because we do not know it.[28]

NOTES

[1] See Sergio Cremaschi, *L'etica del Novecento. Dopo Nietzsche*, ch. 11.

[2] See Henry Sidgwick, *Methods of Ethics* [1874] in *Works*, 15 vols. (Bristol: Thoemmes Press, 1996); Id., *Methods of Ethics* [7th edition: 1907] in *Works*, 15 vols. (Bristol: Thoemmes Press, 1996); see also Sergio Cremaschi, "Sidgwick e il progetto di un'etica scientifica" in *Etica e Politica/Ethics & Politics*, 7/1 (2006), 1–36.

[3] The main ideas are in Friedrich Nietzsche, *Zur genealogie der Moral* [1887] in *Sämtliche Werke, Kritische Studienausgabe*, 15 vols., ed. by Giorgio Colli and Mazzino Montinari (Berlin: de Gruyter, 1980), vol. VI\2, 257–430; Id., *Jenseits von Gut und Böse* [1886] vol. VI\2 of *Sämtliche Werke*.

[4] The fragments of the unfinished work are in Émile Durkheim, *Textes*, ed. by Victor Karady, 3 vols. (Paris: Minuit, 1975), vol. II; the published work that offers most on Durkheim's moral theory is *L'éducation morale* [1925], ed. by Paul Fauconnet (Paris: PUF, 1963); see also William Watts Miller, *Durkheim, Morals and Modernity* (Montreal: McGill – Queen's University Press, 1999); my interpretation of Sidgwick, Nietzsche, and Durkheim is presented in Sergio Cremaschi, *L'etica moderna. Dalla Riforma a Nietzsche* (Rome: Carocci, 2007), chs. 16, 17, and 18.

[5] The main ideas are found in John Dewey, *Outlines of a Critical Theory of Ethics* [1891] in *Early Works (1882–1898)*, 5 vols., ed. by Jo Ann Boydston (Carbondale, Ill: Southern Illinois University Press, 1967–1972), vol. III; *The Study of Ethics: a Syllabus* [1894] in *Early Works (1882–1898)*, vol. IV; John Dewey and James H. Tufts, *Ethics* [1932] in *The Later Works (1925–1953)*, 16 vols. (Carbondale, Ill: Southern Illinois University Press, 1974–89), vol. VII; see also Jennifer Welchman, *Dewey's Ethical Thought* (Ithaca, NY: Cornell University Press, 1997); my interpretation of Dewey is presented in Sergio Cremaschi, *L'etica del Novecento. Dopo Nietzsche*, ch. 1.

[6] See Richard Bernstein, *Beyond Objectivism and Relativism: Science, Hermeneutics, and Praxis* (Philadelphia: University of Pennsylvania Press 1985), 8–16.

[7] David Hume, *An Enquiry concerning Human Understanding* [1748] in *Enquiries*

Concerning Human Understanding and Concerning the Principles of Morals, ed. by Lewis A. Selby-Bigge, Peter H. Nidditch (Oxford: Clarendon, 1975), sect. xii, part 3.

[8] Hans Reichenbach, *The Rise of Scientific Philosophy* (Berkeley Ca: University of California Press, 1951), 319.

[9] Ibidem, 323.

[10] George E. Moore, *Preface* [1922] in *Principia Ethica*, ed. by Thomas Baldwin (Cambridge: Cambridge University Press, 1993), 1–27, particularly 12–16.

[11] Arthur N. Prior, "The Autonomy of Ethics" [1960] in Id., *Papers in Logic and Ethics*, ed. by Peter T. Geach and Anthony I.P. Kenny (London: Duckworth 1976), 88–96.

[12] Henry Poincaré, *Dernières pensées* (Flammarion, Paris 1913), 225.

[13] Karl R. Popper, "What can Logic do for Philosophy?" in *Aristotelian Society. Supplementary Volumes*, 22 (1948), 141–154; Id., *The Open Society and its Enemies* [1945] 2 vols. (London: Routledge, 1966), vol. i, 62–6.

[14] John Searle, "How to derive 'Ought' from 'Is'" in *Philosophical review*, 73 (1964), 43–58; reprint in Id., *Speech Acts* (Cambridge: Cambridge University Press, 1969); cf. W. David Ross, *The Right and the Good* [1930] (Oxford: Clarendon Press, 2002), 32–33; Richard Price, *Review of the Principal Questions of Morals* [1758], ed. by David D. Raphael (Oxford: Clarendon, 1974), 132–3, 155–7.

[15] Karl-Otto Apel, *Das Apriori der Kommunikationsgemeinschaft und die Grudlagen der Ethik*, in *Transformation der Philosophie*, 2 vols. (Frankfurt a.M.: Suhrkamp, 1973), 358–435, particularly 363–370; Ian Rohls, *Geschichte der Ethik* (Mohr: Tübingen, 1991), 443–451.

[16] Henry Sidgwick, *Methods of Ethics*, vol. i, 473.

[17] Charles K. Ogden and, Ivor A. Richards, *The Meaning of Meaning* [1923] (London: Routledge/Thoemmes, 1994), 124–5.

[18] Richard M. Hare, "Imperative Sentences" in *Mind*, 58 (1949), 21–39; Id., *The Language and Morals* [1952] (Oxford: Oxford University Press, 1999).

[19] Apel, *Das Apriori der Kommunikationsgemeinschaft und die Grudlagen der Ethik*, 368.

[20] Adolf Reinach, *Die apriorischen Grundlagen des buergerlichen Rechts* [1913] in Id., *Sämtliche Werke*, 2 vols., ed. by K. Schuhmann, B. Smith (München: Hamden Verlag, 1989), vol. i, 141–278, particularly 169–175, 275–8; see also *Nichtsoziale und soziale Akte* [1911], 355–360.

[21] See Nicolai Hartman, *Ethik* [1926] (Berlin: de Gruyter, 1935), 5–11.

[22] Jean-Paul Sartre, *L'existentialisme est un humanisme* (Paris: Nagel 1946), 77–9.

[23] Popper, *The Open Society and its Enemies*, vol. II, 383–6.

[24] Alasdair MacIntyre, *After Virtue*, (Notre Dame, Ind: University of Notre Dame Press, 1981).

[25] Ibidem.

[26] Ibidem, 10.

[27] On this story see Sergio Cremaschi, "On Analytic and Continental Philosophy" in *Dialogue, Language, Rationality. A Festschrift for Marcelo Dascal*, special issue of *Manuscrito* ed. by Michael B. Wrigley 25/2 (2002), 51–80.

[28] Iris Murdoch (*The Unicorn*, London: Penguin 1963), 100; cf. Ead., *Metaphysics as a Guide to Morals* (Penguin, London 1992), 508.

CHAPTER 2

From the Normative Turn to the Controversy Between Utilitarianism and 'Deontology'

1949–1958: Freeing Moral Discourse From the "Third Person"

In 1949 Stuart Hampshire published a seminal paper where he argued that the opposed trends of emotivism and intuitionism shared a Kantian legacy that was the hidden source of the malaise felt in contemporary moral philosophy. This was the division between moral and factual judgements from which an exclusive interest derived for arguments for accepting moral judgements and accordingly a 'spectatorial' or 'third person' attitude and the blurring of the deliberative dimension of ethical life. Moral judgement is in fact, as argued by Aristotle, 'deliberation,' a procedure quite different from those followed in the exact sciences, where not only the truth of a judgment, but also the circumstance that it is somebody who expresses it, is something that matters. Thus moral judgements are not arbitrary judgements as assumed by the emotivists; they are just not as rigorous as scientific ones. Thus Moore's intuitionism and emotivism are two *frères ennemis* who endlessly quarrel by affirming or denying the same thesis. The original mistake on which moral philosophy rests is the requirement that the relevant judgement be the one of the impartial spectator, not the one of the agent, a bequest to contemporary ethics from utilitarianism and Kantian ethics.[1]

1958: From Moore's Anti-naturalism to Anscombe's, Geach's and Foot's Anti-anti-naturalism

Towards the end of the fifties, as a result of the attempt to introduce themes from Wittgentein's philosophy into ethics or as side-effects of developments in logic and philosophy of language that had gone beyond

35

the philosophical ideas available to Moore in 1903, several arguments limiting the allegedly destructive consequences first of the naturalistic fallacy and then of Hume's law started being formulated. The first proponents of such arguments were called sometimes neo-naturalists, not because they were materialists or proponents of any program of reduction of ethics to the natural sciences, but just because they denied Moore's negation, which in turn was not accurately described as anti-naturalist, since he himself admitted that it was best described as anti-naturalist-and-metaphysical.

Elisabeth Anscombe in a famous paper worked out a criticism of modern moral philosophy as a whole (not just twentieth-century Anglo-Saxon philosophy as Hampshire had done) attacking the primacy of rules and obligatory action shared by Kant and Bentham, and vindicating the main element of Aristotelian ethics, dispositions or virtues.[2]

Philippa Foot argued that evaluative expressions connected with virtues and vices, as "rude" and "courageous" have factual criteria of application and there are premises from which, in virtue of the descriptive meaning of such terms, conclusions such as "thus he behaved in a rude way" are logically justified while being evaluative judgments; that is, there are circumstances under which the shift from "is" to "ought" is legitimised.[3] Starting with this conclusion, a criticism to Kant is formulated. Kant was a psychological hedonist and was accordingly unable to conceive of the possibility of moral behaviour without something like the categorical imperative; the latter instead is useless in so far as a moral person cares for ends such as other people's good, and behaves morally because s/he wants to reach such ends, and accordingly pursues hypothetical, not categorical imperatives.[4]

Peter Geach carried out a similar criticism against the naturalistic fallacy argument starting with the existence of a plurality of meanings of "good" and the unjustified identification of all meanings with its moral meaning.[5]

1958: Baier's Way From Metaethics to Normative Ethics:

Another break of the non-cognitivist siege around the "ought" was carried out by another of the post-Wittgensteinian currents, namely the "good reasons approach." This was started in the early fifties by Stephen Toulmin by leaving the early-Wittgensteinian and Logical Empiricist way provided by analysis of the meaning of moral terms and taking instead the late-Wittgensteinian way provided by analysis of the structure of arguments. Toulmin's still Wittgensteinian outlook was that morality is a life-form in which we are always already engaged, and accordingly no argument is possible with the immoralist and any argument is possible only with partners who share one given *LebensForm*, with the 'prospectivist' implications of such a commitment that make Toulmin's ethics look like a tempered form of relativism.[6] Thus, Toulmin's approach would apparently not have run against the stream prevailing in the fifties were it not for a pupil who, as often happens with pupils who take masters too seriously, turned the outcome upside down. The decisive point was the claim that argument is possible in favour of the very "moral point of view" as such, a general point of view where all more determined *LebensFormen* bearing each one particular morality are included.

One basic claim on which the argument rests is the primacy of moral reasons over reasons of different kinds, for

> the very *raison d'être* of a morality is to yield reasons which overrule the reasons of self-interest in those cases when everyone's following self-interest would be harmful to everyone. Hence moral reasons are superior to all others.[7]

The other is the claim that it is possible to derive reasons for acting morally from egoistic reasons, since it is in the interest of every rational agent that a system of overarching reasons be enforced in order to solve conflicts of interests, and such reasons have to overrule other reasons on the basis of their very function qua moral reasons; in other words, a Hobbesian agent will have reasons for behaving as a Kantian agent, or adoption of a system of rules overruling everyone's interest is in the interest of everyone alike, even if "following the rules of a morality is not of course identical with following self-interest."[8] One implication of Baier's argument is that metaethics is not ethically neutral, or that metaethical considerations are enough in order to justify absolute morality, or the moral point of view as such, or the claim that at least a few among the existing positive moralities are not superstition and prejudice or sets of irrational commands accepted on authority, but instead may be rationally justified. Another implication is that egoism – that is, Sidgwick's open possibility of rational egoism alternative to universal hedonism, and its Nietzschean counterpart, immoralism – is not an available option, but can be refuted on rational arguments; that is, the moral point of view is to be adopted compulsorily.

1958: Lewis's Discovery of Apel's Performative Contradiction

Clarence Irvin Lewis, one of the authors of the American reception of Logical Empiricism and a second-generation Pragmatist worked out a theory of value within the framework of his own "conceptual pragmatism."[9] His main claims are that – against emotivism and intuitionism – value judgements may be true or false and valuation is a kind of empirical knowledge, since the eventual foundation of all values is hedonistic, granted that the basic value is a subjective experience of "satisfaction."[10] His ethics was both "naturalistic" and "rationalistic," since, on the one hand, the rightness of an action cannot be established in a way independent from the goodness of its consequences, and good and evil are empirical facts[11], but also, on the other hand, "right or wrong cannot be determined unless with reference to rules or principles."[12] Prudence is a first step in the direction of rationality, and the imperative to respect other people's interests as we would like others to respect our own may be introduced on the basis of prudence and an ability to generalize. This is achieved on the basis of a fundamental imperative that does not require any reason because by denying it one would fall into contradiction. It prescribes: "be consistent in valuation and in thought and action."[13] The act of denying such prescription would be self-vanifying, and would instantiate what Lewis calls a "pragmatic contradiction."[14] In this way Lewis too introduces a Kantian element into ethics with an argument that 14 years later will be repeated in a modified form by Karl-Otto Apel.

1966: Searle's Infringement of Hume's Law

In the sixties, after the demise of the naturalistic fallacy argument, Hume's law also came unavoidably under attack.[15] Besides papers by Arthur N. Prior and Max Black,[16] the best known argument is the one by Searle on promises by which he tries to prove that a shift from a descriptive statement such as "John has uttered the words: I promise to give Smith five dollars'" to the prescriptive statement "John owes Smith five dollars" is logically justified.[17] The point on which Searle's argument rests is the existence of "institutional facts," a category of facts where promises stand as a paramount example, where the "ought" is embedded within the "is" from the very beginning. The argument as such is less novel than Searle believed, since promises were the traditional intuitionist's hobby-horse, and they were used as an example of a case where a foundation for obligation is provided by a fact by Richard Price, William Whewell, and David Ross.

1960–1983: The Continental Normative Turn and the Rehabilitation of Practical Philosophy

At about the same time, that is around the year Gadamer's *Truth and Method* was published, a parallel movement also started in Germany, from Heideggerian hermeneutical amoralism to the so-called rehabilitation of practical philosophy, firstly on an epistemological ground, then in normative ethics. Aristotle's practical philosophy is described in *Truth and Method* as the best example of an hermeneutic process. Aristotle's *phronesis* aims at solving the problem of "application," applying a general category to one particular situation, the third step of interpretation for hermeneutics, after comprehension and explanation. This is what highlights the difference between *phronesis* and *techne*, for moral knowledge is possible only facing concrete cases, since the good show up only in particular situations.[18] Such moral knowledge is not a normative ethics and cannot give answers to particular questions, since its task is limited to helping moral consciousness in its effort at self-clarification. Such moral knowledge is accordingly a kind of discourse that follows a different logic from the objectifying methods of modern science, in so far as first it is not objective knowledge and second, unlike *techne*, it cannot be learned and unlearned and cannot be 'applied.' Aristotle's enormous merit has been that of foreshadowing the impasse into which our scientific culture is caught by its description of practical reason as distinguished from theoretical reason and technical ability, and "the concept of *praxis* of the last two centuries has been a horrible deformation [...] an application of science to technical tasks."[19] The apparently shared ideal in the fifties was that of a society where the impossible task of exempting us from genuinely practical decisions is entrusted to specialists.[20] What we need is a recovery of the dimension of moral comprehension, a dimension distinguished from others by its historical and dialogical character. Genuine praxis, as exemplified by practices such as jurisprudence, is not application of an abstract rule, and it is a mistaken comprehension of what praxis is, and accordingly of the relationship of theory and praxis, which lies at the root of the present deadlock making ethics impossible. Indeed the ancient view of knowledge assumed theory to be something which already implied the shift to praxis, while for modern philosophy a theory is an explanation of phenomena such as to make their technical control possible. It was from such an outlook that caricatures of ethics such as Kantian ethics derived.[21] Aristotle provides an alternative to the conundrums generated by Enlightenment ethics by suggesting that this should not be a theory to be put into practice, since moral knowledge, first, is not something different from the awareness of the rule shared by everybody, second, it includes the dimension of "application" to the individual case and, thirdly, being *phronesis*, is itself a moral virtue.[22]

40

The rehabilitation of practical philosophy was the name of a movement in German philosophy that started around 1970 and whose authors were neo-Aristotelians such as Joachim Ritter, various kinds of neo-Kantians such as Apel, Habermas, Paul Lorenzen, Oswald Schwemmer, Friedrich Kambartel and others, partly Aristotelian partly Hegelian, such as Manfred Riedel and Karl-Heinz Ilting.[23] The shared element was a refusal of technocratic political and social sciences and a vindication of a role for philosophy as such. Only in the aftermath of the discussion did clearly articulated proposals for a revival of normative ethics begin to emerge. Neo-Aristotelians such as Joachim Ritter argued that the tradition of practical philosophy started with Aristotle, reached its apex with Christian Wolff and dissolved with Kant,[24] at the time when, as a result of separation of ethics from politics, practical philosophy turned into a weakened version of itself, ethics, consisting of a system of postulates and imperatives of pure will that are relevant only to the inner sphere, and which is reduced to a theory of morality, separated from "legality." Hegel's concept of *Sittlichkeit* in a sense first recovered the institutional dimension of ethics in the Aristotelian sense. Among Ritter's pupils, Ottfried Höffe tried to combine Aristotle and Kant,[25] and Joachim Spaemann stressed Thomist accents in his Aristotelianism by emphasizing the notion of nature.[26] Among Gadamer's pupils, Rüdiger Bubner tried to combine hermeneutic motifs with themes from Anglo-Saxon philosophy of action.[27] Manfred Riedel, less clearly definable as an Aristotelian, suggested, instead of a recovery of practical philosophy that he believed was impossible after Kant's dissolution of "metaphysics," an inquiry into a domain that he dubbed "metapolitics," the exploration of metaphysical principles at the root of ways of conceptualising politics.[28]

1960–1983: The Continental Normative Turn and Discourse Ethics

The most famous among the German vindications of Normative ethics was Apel's program for a discourse ethics. Apel's claims, as formulated in the 1972 paper that started the trend of discourse ethics, were the following: a) the moral point of view is not the subject-matter of a decision; b) a few basic contents of normative ethics are justified by transcendental arguments; c) Pragmatism provides the missing link between analytic philosophy and Existentialism, which are both theories of the impossibility of normative discourse sharing a drastic separation of fact and value; the notion of pragmatic contradiction – which, as I argued, was discovered by the pragmatist Clarence I. Lewis – provides a ground for refuting any refusal of the moral point of view; d) the pragmatic dimension of language as discovered first by Charles Sanders Peirce, the father of Pragmatism, provides a way of turning around the fact-value division in so far as there are contradictions – of a performative nature, not of syntactic nature – in any immoralist or fanatic or totalitarian doctrine, and the unveiling of such contradictions provides a rational basis for minimal imperatives of a universalist ethics of responsibility and emancipation.[29]

Apel's ideas were popularised and inserted into a more ambitious and systematic enterprise of: Re-Kantianizing Marxism by Habermas and his school in the eighties. The time, the decade of the so-called Crisis of Marxism ending in 1989 by the fall of the Berlin wall, was perfect for granting a wide echo to Habermas's attempt in those countries where Marxism had been until recently an institutionalized current of thought, and the Habermasian school seemed to provide a proxy for a no longer available coherent, if not consistent, system of leftist ideas.

What Habermas had to contribute of his own was a quest for an answer to the question "what went wrong" or what was the source of the "pathologies of modernity" that paved the way to Nazism, which had been the great question to which his master Adorno had found only elusive answers. In order to modify Adorno's answer, which relied on Weber's pessimistic diagnosis of the "iron cage" of modern techno-scientific mentality (what Heidegger called the *Gestell*), he looked to Weber for an alternative theory of "rationalization" that differentiates kinds of societies according to their mechanisms of coordination, adding the idea that modern society differs from traditional communities not only because of the coming of instrumental rationality but also because of the adoption of reflexive codes of behaviour inspired by rational and universal principles.[30]

He also added a contribution from Oxford philosophy and pragmatism, namely the idea of communication as being the basis of language with a dialogical use of the latter as the standard option and its monological use as a "limiting case."[31] Communicative action aimed at reaching the same agreement is the normal procedure, and such action is the source of the validity of norms (always presupposed as given). Such a validity results from procedures, it is the validity of the norm supported by better arguments in a situation where no coercion is exerted apart form the inner constraints deriving form the structure of communication itself.[32]

1936–1981: Utilitarianism Redivivus

After Moore, utilitarianism seemed definitely defeated as an ethical doctrine, while it was more alive than ever in other disciplines, primarily economics, without too much discussion of its justification qua philosophical doctrine. Curiously enough, as early as 1936, that is in the heyday of emotivism, a path-breaking attempt was made to give utilitarianism a fresh life. Significantly, it was carried out by an economist, Roy Harrod. It was published in one of the most prestigious journals but had no deep impact among philosophers, at least for a few years. The ideas discussed in the paper came to the fore in a discussion that was lively, albeit confined to a restricted circle, in the fifties. Harrod's two innovations were on two points: a) the definition of 'the good': not pleasure or happiness but just preferences are to be considered, in order to avoid heavy assumptions on such issues as the possibility of knowing inner states of other minds; b) the definition of 'the right': not the maximising individual act, but the rule which would maximise satisfaction of preferences should be adopted as a criterion for the right.[33] This is, in Harrod's words, a 'Kantian' utilitarianism that enjoys the assets of not being at variance with everyday morality and not requiring implausible theoretical assumptions.

In the discussion of the fifties the label 'rule utilitarianism' was adopted instead of Harrod's label.[34] The discussion weighed the pros and cons of rule vs. act utilitarianism, and soon came to distinguish between an *ideal* rule utilitarianism and a *real* rule utilitarianism.[35] The dispute was closed by David Lyons's proof of the extensional equivalence of rule and act utilitarianism, once consequences far enough are taken into account by the latter, that is, an act-utilitarian with sufficient information and ability to process such information would prescribe or prohibit precisely the same acts as a rule utilitarian would, or, again in other words, even an act-utilitarian has reasons not to accept the 'repugnant conclusion.'[36]

The discussion, which was restricted to a close circle made by scholars of utilitarianism, prepared the materialism for the new boom of utilitarianism as a normative ethics as soon as the normative turn was on the agenda. The most successful example was Hare. Having been one leading figure in the heyday of non-cognitivist metaethics, he was able to recycle himself into the leading figure of an updated version of utilitarian normative ethics from the early seventies without apparently disowning his own non-cognitivism. His new doctrine adopts rule-utilitarianism, after having admitted of its theoretical uselessness as a practical device for everyday-life decision, as a token for the 'true' theory. But the latter is an ideal act-utilitarianism that plays the part of the argument for justifying a system of prescription and then disappears forever, since it is impossible in practice to apply it to whatsoever situation, given any human being's limited information, limited computing ability, and proneness to self-deception.[37] That is, a would-be act utilitarian calculus would provide a justification for recommending that the mass (Hare is snobbish and cynical enough to call it the *proles*, echoing George Orwell, but having enough nerve to adopt Orwell's 'inner-party'-member point of view) follow rule-utilitarian prescriptions, that is Sidgwick's "common-sense morality." And in a perfectly Sidgwickian elitist spirit, Hare adds that limited exceptions may be made for the thinking elite, that is academics, who could make educated guesses about the advantages of transgressing a rule from time to time without letting people know. This is, Hare believes, a Kantian version of utilitarianism, or a point where an intelligent Kantian and an intelligent utilitarian would meet.[38]

Richard Brandt's version of an updated utilitarian doctrine was less successful but also much more sophisticated than Hare's. Brandt's main idea is to keep utilitarianism only as a device for evaluating moral codes taken as wholes. What should be assessed is the utility of a generalized compliance with the code in a society, where a certain percentage of compliance is taken, on empirical or conventional grounds, as a definition of "generalized" acceptance.[39] Such an approach avoids many of the difficulties of classical utilitarianism without lapsing into the triviality of real rule utilitarianisms, Hare's included, since it keeps an evaluative function to the principle of utility while taking a sophisticated view of how moral codes work in cultures. It is not by accident that Brandt also did valuable anthropological field-work.[40] The weakest point in Brandt's account, albeit more sensible than Hare's, is the most philosophical one, namely the problem of the final justification of the adoption of a moral code. This is passed round by Brandt by the sensible consideration that it is roughly desirable for everybody to live in a society with a moral code and the most informed persons will desire for themselves and their children life in a society with a code closer to the ideal one, simply for reasons of interest, but this would bring such reasons closer to those that could be adopted in a kind of deliberative procedure by someone who would have the general interest of the members of society in mind.[41] The argument is quite reasonable but also disappointing, amounting to the conclusion that in order to be a reasonable utilitarian one may simply become a more traditional character, say a Kantian or an Aristotelian.

Hare and Brandt's were the two most significant attempts at providing comprehensive utilitarian views taking all criticism to act utilitarianism and to the hedonist theory of the good into account. Another important attempt was John Harsanyi's rational choice version of a preference-based rule-utilitarianism. Yet, Harsanyi's was a development in a different direction, that is the direction of a technically sophisticated theory of collective decisions that could help in clarifying discussion of such issues and freeing them from rhetoric and sentimentalism (as Harsanyi's decisive criticism of Rawls's *maximin* criterion proved), but taking the basic philosophical issues for settled, on the basis of shared common-sense assumptions. For example, Harsanyi adopted rule-utilitarianism while being aware of the criticism it had attracted, simply because it comes closer to common sense, and indeed because the choice between rule and act goes beyond the scope of his rational-choice approach.[42]

An intriguing phenomenon was the revival of a popular version of utilitarianism as a real-world movement for moral reform, pointing to the spreading of a 'new morality' as the goal to be pursued. The fight against the so-called Paradigm of the Sacrality of Life seems to summarize the goals of this current, led by Peter Singer, and after him Helga Kuhse and James Rachels.[43] The current was, and still is, quite active in the field of bioethics, engaged in battles for controversial goals including involuntary euthanasia and infanticide of severely handicapped children. Apparently the focus of the current is more a Benthamite original project for a secular morality than the specific utilitarian theoretical claims. In fact, even if Hare was Singer's master, the theoretical structure of the doctrines adopted seems to be less of interest than their effectiveness and impact on public discourse; for example, a negative anti-suffering criterion of the good is adopted without much discussion of its theoretical difficulties, just because of its moral appeal, and act utilitarianism is kept, after all criticism it has undergone, because it looks like the only available basis for the argument for drastic moral reform.[44]

The following remarks may be appropriate: a) utilitarianism *qua* ethical doctrine had been a discredited doctrine for a few decades after Sidgwick and Moore; b) it has enjoyed a new life since the fifties, when it still seemed a matter of rather antiquarian interest; the reasons for such a rebirth have been, on the one hand, theoretical, that is a process of self-immunisation from criticism by reducing original claims, and on the other, practical, that is, need for techniques of decision on practical issues after the new start of public discussion in the sixties; c) the practical reasons for the revival tended to two diverging outcomes: on the one hand to Harsanyi's rational-choice utilitarianism that ends up with a philosophically neutral machinery for treating public decisions, on the other, to a theoretically rather uncritical version of 'negative act utilitarianism' because of practical needs and ideological commitments that made it look plausible enough to that part of public opinion that wanted a secular moral *doctrine*, no matter how sophisticated, so long as it was drastically *secular*.

1971–1998: A Resurrection of Several Kinds of 'Deontological' Ethics

After Baier, a 'deontological' front reappeared at the very moment the idea of a viable normative ethics was proposed again. Such as front had disappeared between the thirties and the sixties as a consequence of Ross's checkmate, self-inflicted by his admission of the impossibility to establish priority criteria between different duties in the concrete case. The alignment was scattered, since right theories such as Dworkin's, Nozick's, Gewirth's shared a few motifs with Kantian ethics and Rawls's theory shared others, while Thomas Nagel's doctrine, albeit dependent on the *good reasons approach* was a more traditional kind of ethical theory by far closer to Kant's than any of the former. Besides, the Anglo-Saxon nineteenth-century background was intuitionism, the doctrine for which Sidgwick coined the term deontology (actually taking Bentham's neologism for 'private ethics' and applying it to anti-Benthamite doctrines). A most naïve move was Rawls's adoption of the label 'deontological' for his own theory, without realizing that it was one more waste-paper basket category created by consequentialists as a cage for their own opponents,[45] an unfortunate move that helped to spread confusion over three decades of discussion.

What happened was that a number of currents unavoidably rescued

47

one or another item from the tradition of 'old' moral theory preceding the Benthamite dream of a 'new' morality, and were thus unavoidably linked to one or another aspect of Kantian ethics, that was a summary, or rationalization of such tradition. But also ideas about Kant's own historically given theories were incredibly vague in the Anglo-Saxon academia at the time of the normative turn.

The result of Rawls's attempt at finding an alternative to utilitarian theories of justice was in fact, more than a 'Kantian' doctrine, a sort of modified intuitionism applied to a limited area within ethics, that is, public ethics. His only modification to intuitionist theory was the introduction of a 'lexicographic' ordering of principles in order to avoid unranked pluralism that made Ross's and Prichard's intuitionism an impracticable approach. It is this ranking of different principles the trait that makes Rawls's theory a 'deontological' one, in so far as it allows for summing up such disparate items as freedom, rights and material welfare within one magnitude to be maximized. It is not very much for qualifying as a 'Kantian' theory, and yet in 1971 Rawls presented his own doctrine as a 'Kantian' doctrine by advancing a "Kantian interpretation of the person" as the 'moral psychology' adopted by the 'contracting parties' in his model of a social contract, and suggesting that this model may be a new version of the Kantian idea of the categorical imperative.[46] In 1980 he added that his contracting parties are no egoists, but instead 'rational persons' who have as a primary interest their own self-respect as autonomous subjects who try to bring into reality their own conception of the good.[47] Besides he added later that Kantian ethics is different from intuitionism in so far as it is anti-realist, not having 'moral facts' to discover but being instead a constructive procedure for creating, instead of discovering, moral facts, in a way which expresses the moral essence of subjects. Indeed the main difficulty, not to say mistake, in his theory of 1971, that is lack of reasons for adopting such an implausible criterion as the *maximin* should be allegedly dissolved by the consideration that the theory is not backed by an empirical psychology, which would admit of some propensity to risk, and is based instead only on a 'moral psychology,' which specifies the most reasonable conception of a person compatible with the known facts about human nature and accordingly trying to base the theory of justice on rational choice theory had been just "a mistake."[48]

Ronald Dworkin, Richard Nozick and Alan Gewirth between the seventies and the nineties published a number of contributions where comprehensive theories of social justice were developed as alternatives both to Rawls's and to utilitarian theories.[49] The shared element was the fact of starting with a theory of individual rights and developing an outline of a just social structure by deriving social regulations from rights. The remarkable element in one of such approaches, Gewirth's, was an attempt at crossing the border between metaethics and normative ethics through his 'generic consistency principle' or at 'founding' normative ethics in a rationalistic mood close to Baier's.[50]

A family of across-the-Atlantic relatives was the New Frankfurt School launched by Apel and Habermas that proposed a transcendentally based public-sphere human-rights philosophy. This was Kantian ethics in a more direct sense than any of the former, and yet it shared some strange enough features with Rawls and the rights-theorists, that is, the division between public morality and private or community-based overall conceptions of the good, and a serious problem in the moment of application of moral principles to concrete cases. This difficulty was raised by Albrecht Wellmer against Habermas, and recent developments of Habermas's theory, in *Between Facts and Norms*, may be accounted for as (I believe unsuccessful) attempts at paving Wellmer's objections.[51] If these hold, what needs bringing in is the Kantian theory of judgement, the doctrine Hannah Arendt stressed in her political philosophy, but this opens the way for that merging 'Kantian' theory with various kinds of 'Aristotelian' theory which has been taking place from the nineties and which is mentioned in what follows.

The most genuinely Kantian moral philosopher has been perhaps somebody who has been comparatively an outsider, that is Alan Donagan, with his Kantianised natural law theory. Donagan's main point was that Kantian ethics was ethics without qualification, or that the ancient Stoics, Cicero, the Christian and Jewish medieval writers had argued one idea, the existence of a basic imperative, respect for persons, that does not even need a 'foundation' in the sense of Baier or Gewirth, since the burden of proof lies on those who, like the utilitarians, want to subvert the old morality and justify a new morality; until further notice, or until the utilitarians have provided a satisfying proof, the old view of the moral law as 'natural' (that is, valid previous to enactment by any authority, secular or religious) law has a weighty justification of a coherentist kind, because of its ability to account for a tradition of moral thinking that has lasted and has been refined though centuries.[52]

A strange bed-fellow to Kantian doctrines is the New Natural Law theory, the only current for which the label 'deontological' as created by consequentalists may prove convincing. In fact John Finnis's is a (physical) natural law with (casuistic) rigourism, that is an apparently neo-Thomist theory. Most decent neo-Thomists tried to stress either the virtue ethics dimensions or the quasi-Kantian structure of the derivation of moral duties from the practical (non-moral) principle of "synderesis" (*bonum faciendum, malum vitandum*) which is presented as a self-evident transcendental principle.[53] On the contrary Finnis tried to prove the existence of unconditional (particular) imperatives and the unchanging character of a law written in the world order, which reverses brilliantly the order of priority established by Donagan's reading of the natural law tradition, where persons came first.[54]

The New Controversy Between Utilitarians and Kantians and the Emergence of a Third Way

Words have a story of their own, often dissociated from the story of things in themselves. So, not unlike a *suisse* is in France a door-keeper (of any nationality), and a *portoghese* is in Italy a free-rider (most of the time of Italian nationality) so in the United States a *Kantian* has been now for a few decades a proponent of rights-based theories, of intuitionism, or of any theoretical item that could be fit for some reason for the waste-paper basket of 'deontology.'

On the other hand, Anscombe's invention of the *word* consequentialism came some time after the dissolution of the *thing* 'utilitarianism' into a disunited family of doctrines making room for maximizing considerations in the assessment of actions, policies etc. The family is so loose that on one extreme one finds extremely technical elaborations such as those by John Harsanyi where the point is assessing issues in terms of rational choice theory, a pursuit about which there cannot be any room for philosophical disagreement, and on the other extreme one finds rule-utilitarian considerations by a number of quite sensible authors – one out of many is Barry Brian – who do a wonderful job on individual topics, in terms about which no 'Kantian' may have any reason of principle for disagreement. The sore point may be that rule-utilitarians are so sensible on applied issues as to be hardly distinguished from Kantians but keep on being sensible also on foundational issues and have nothing to say on issues such as "why be moral" or "does one have internal reasons for acting morally" for which their answer is that one already has to have a benevolent attitude *before* adopting a utilitarian ethics, which sounds like a vicious circle.[55]

Between these two allegedly opposed fronts an interesting controversy arose during the seventies and eighties that was on the one hand an unaware re-enactment of the nineteenth-century controversy between utilitarians and intuitionists,[56] on the other the first 'real' occasion for a confrontation between Kantian ethics and utilitarianism, since in nineteenth-century England Kantian ethics was still virtually unknown, and then it was the occasion for the emergence of an alleged third party, virtue-ethics, which in turn was no real third party since it was a highly composite phenomenon and perhaps not primarily a different normative ethic but an attempt at 'shuffling,' or re-defining issues. The discussion concentrated on the following points. The first was recourse to intuitions by (alleged) Kantians and its justification. Intuitions, after having been used by Ross and Prichard, had disappeared from the discussion since the thirties, as a result of the 'victory' by emotivists in the controversy with neo-intuitionists. They had been brought back again by Rawls. From the consequentialist front the attack concentrated on identification between intuitions and culturally and sociologically determined prejudices, basically the same argument used by John Stuart Mill against William Whewell.[57] The counter-attack lay in development of more refined coherentist approaches trying to show how much can be reached though reflective-equilibrium procedures, and how much top-down strategies require of heavy assumptions while yielding less than coherentist strategies.[58] The result of the counter-attack has been reviving interest in intuitionism, even if the proposals for recovery that have been developed point to several directions, not particularly Kantian in their normative outcomes.[59]

Another topic has been the so-called repugnant conclusion, or the alleged utilitarian defence of Machiavellianism or of the unqualified lesser evil.[60] The strategy has been that of insulating the trouble by a distinction between act-utilitarianism and rule-utilitarianism, allegedly immune from the criticism or, by consequent act-utilitarians, proving that in the long run, when distant consequences are considered, also actions of which some crude Machiavellian attitude would approve would be condemned by consequent act-utilitarianism. This defence was made possible by Lyons's proof of the extensional equivalence of act- and rule-utilitarianism and lies at the root of Hare's two-tiered model that makes act and rule utilitarianism compatible. Those who adopted such a line of argument, though, should have been more consistent in admitting of no room for moral reform by utilitarian theory, since the argument ends with the conclusion that no exception may be admitted to any rule (a conclusion that Hare did not adopt drastically enough). The most striking detail in Lyon's proof, yet, is the circumstance that it repeats a famous argument provided, before Bentham, by the *priest*

William Paley, an uneasy bed-fellow for utilitarians, who had argued that the rightness of actions depends on their consequences and yet no unjust action has really good consequences, once we also take distant and indirect consequences into account.[61]

Another, and indeed the one with the heaviest impact, has been the idea of justice. The very *raison d'être* of Rawls's theory was providing an alternative to the utilitarian theory of justice, which was strictly no theory of justice at all since it merged justice into total or average welfare. It is because of his refusal to adopt a theory that could justify oppression of minorities by majorities that Rawls classified his own theory by the somewhat dubious label of 'deontological.'[62]

One related topic has been the notion of human rights, an enormously popular topic after the UN declarations of human rights shortly after World War II and the target of endless attacks by utilitarians. The most moderate line has been Hare's, reducing 'rights' to a derivate concept, a convenient summary or reminder for some list of preferences to be satisfied which, for a number of reasons, may be given priority over other preferences.[63] Hard-liners, that is act-utilitarians led by Peter Singer, kept denouncing human rights as a dangerous myth, a myth which blinds us before obvious facts, such as that enormous masses of happiness have been produced more effectively in countries such as post-Maoist China where the job has been done a little bit wholesale, without paying too much attention to western niceties such as aversion to the death-penalty and care for freedom in reproductive choices.

At the turn of the seventies, several outsiders joined the controversy, and indeed the most memorable disputes between utilitarians and anti-utilitarians have involved precisely these outsiders, that at some time came under the label of virtue-theorists, even if the label was tight enough as not to leave out such a prominent figure as Amartya Sen and to look disappointing for such a rich body of ideas as Bernard Williams's. And yet, the feeling was widespread that a new heterogeneous company, made of so-called virtue ethicists, had entered the stage, whose most popular characters were MacIntyre and Bernard Williams, and then Michael Stocker, Annette Baier, Martha Nussbaum, with her *sputnik* Sen gravitating along a somewhat eccentric, half-Aristotelian and half-Kantian orbit. The targets of their attacks have been primarily:

a) on a more applied level, the anomaly by which ethics after Rawls tended to become a discussion of *public* issues, leaving most of the standard subject-matter of ethical discussion in a limbo, that of conceptions of 'the good' adopted by individuals or communities, and for some reason unfit for rational discussion on the basis of *public* reasons; the attacks have been centred on the idea that the dichotomy between *public ethics* (that Habermas called 'morality,' the Hegelian *Moralität*) and *private ethics* (individual and communitarian, that Habermas called 'ethics,' that is the Hegelian *Sittlichkeit*) is flawed by an uncritical assumption with no theoretical backing, the dichotomy between a public sphere and a private sphere, that is taken from the sociological contingencies of modern western societies and uplifted to the heaven of philosophical categories without passing any examination.[64]

b) on a historico-philosophical level, the attack has focused on the diagnosis of a shared ground between utilitarianism and Kantian ethics, both suffering from the shared malaise of modern moral philosophy, that is a restricted view of the tasks of ethics, confined to discussion of obligatory actions while forgetting the wider range of dimensions of action that were examined under the Greek label of *aretè*, improperly translated by *virtue* and meaning originally *excellence*.[65]

After 25 years of discussion, it is far from clear whether virtue ethics is one trend. The most alarming symptom for the health of the school in the next decades is the reaction by one Kantian trend, at both the historiographic and the theoretical level, aimed at encapsulating all the virtue-ethics good reasons within a Kantian approach, by proving first of all that Kant's 'real' ethics, was actually a kind of virtue ethics centred on 'judgement.'[66] Is virtue ethics the third trend of normative ethics? One might answer that there have been two disparate currents of critics of Kantian ethics and of critics of utilitarianism,[67] or that there is little to share between the strongly realist and in his last phase biologico-naturalist version of MacIntyre's virtue ethics or the realist adoption of a detailed account of human nature as a basis for normativity by Martha Nussbaum,[68] and Williams's moderately sceptical argument against the theory of obligatory action.[69] Best of all, one may suggest that virtue ethics is not a name for a current in normative ethics. There has been indeed also a side-phenomenon of virtue ethics qua normative ethics, in the form of literature describing and recommending the list of virtues appropriate for the active citizen, the righteous physician, the caring nurse, but this has been a rather sugary rivulet beside the main stream. The mainstream has been a whirling flow of contributions discussing the flaws and the persisting dogmas in the reasons for the 1958 normative turn, and 'virtue ethics' is most of all a signpost for this flow of literature.

Onora O'Neill, one of Rawls's pupils, went one step beyond her master by proposing a truly Kantian overall moral theory instead of Rawls's limited one, by denying the neat division between justice and virtue that had been made explicit in the course of the discussion between the 'Kantians' and the 'virtue theorists' in the eighties. O'Neill challenged the assumption that only justice may be universal and virtue is bound to be particular and relative if it be comprehensive and substantive. The hidden dogma shared by both fronts was in this instance that abstraction is not idealization, or particularity is not relativism, that is, it is possible to come closer to actual communities with their own cultures and practices and to criticize, reform, or enact moral judgements on the life of such communities without abandoning universal standards, because what matters is not universality but instead universalizability, and we may accordingly agree rationally on a highly specific set of norms that may be enforced only within one given community without dismissing our claims to universally valid justification of our claims.[70] Other authors, among them Christine Korsgaaard, Marcia Baron, Nancy Sherman and Barbara Herman, worked along similar lines, discovering the shared element between Kantian and Aristotelian ethics and detecting the room for virtues and emotions within the Kantian ethics.[71]

Theoretical and Practical Reasons for the Revival of Practical Philosophy

Let me try to sum up. There has been an astonishing parallel revival of normative ethics after the *annus mirabilis* 1958 in two separate philosophical worlds. *Nihil fit sine causa*, and the normative turn also had a number of causes. They were of two different orders, one theoretical and the other, not surprisingly, 'practical' or better social and political. The first order of causes, coming top-down from theory, were:

a) first of all, elaborations by second-generation pupils on the premises established by masters: the main example is Wittgensteinian philosophy that in its first version seemed the best formulation of two tragic outlooks, either moral nihilism or moral mysticism, both of them quite on a par with the *Zeitgeist* of the finis Austriae, and in its second version seemed a formulation of an absolutely non-tragic and mild attitude of para-relativism (in fact prospectivism, which is in one sense almost the opposite), quite on a par with the Oxbridge mood, but which in the hands of a first-generation pupil such as Toulmin revealed its potentialities for a perhaps slightly inconclusive, and yet far from vacuous, discourse on moralities, and in the hands of a second-generation pupil (ironically another Austrian), Baier, provided an argument to the fact that *any* moral code is non-negotiable by its very definition and function *qua* moral code; Baier has not often been quoted by Anglo-Saxon philosophers, with the notable exception of his pupil Stephen Darwall,[72] first of all by Rawls who owed him much more than he was aware of, and is totally unknown in Europe, his being an Austrian *émigré* notwithstanding;

b) the legacy of intuitionist critique to consequentialism, that is, the legacy of Whewell's objections to Bentham and Mill, incorporated by Sidgwick in what he meant to be a refutation of intuitionism and was actually the starting-point of Moore's and Ross's weakened neo-intuitionism, on non-consequentialist reasons for action in cases such as those of promises and truth-telling, on the impossibility of a monist definition of the good etc.; this legacy has emerged again, with Rawls and others, two or three decades after the apparent defeat of the neo-intuitionists by the emotivists, albeit with no awareness of the sources for the ideas that were being put at stake;

c) an historico-theoretical reason, namely revision of Hegelian and utilitarian caricature of Kantian ethics and of Hegelian and Continental caricatures of utilitarianism, gradual demise on the Continent of Hegelian Philosophies, from the crisis of Italian neo-idealism around 1938 to the crisis of Marxism in the eighties, that had been providing powerful reasons for not reasoning in ethical terms;

d) a parallel historico-theoretical reason, namely revision of an anti-Enlightenment attitude on the Continent that had its roots in bad historical reconstructions that were gradually dismantled by historians of ideas, in Political prejudices, such as the identification of the Enlightenment with the bourgeoisie and Capitalism or in religious prejudices such as Catholic anti-Modernism; the U-turn which took place between Adorno and Habermas with regard to their attitude to the Enlightenment is enlightening.

The second order of causes that came down-top from society were arguments discussed in a sustained way in public opinion in western countries: resistance to American armed intervention in Vietnam and the right of citizens to disobey, the civil rights movements, in Germany discussion of the *Schuldfrage* after the end of World War II, later on, in a few European countries, discussion of the morality of politics in connection with the emergence of terrorist groups, and in both America and Europe the discussion about the redefinition of the means and ends of political action, equality, individual freedom coming with feminist movements. In the same years growing complexity of biomedical practice and growing awareness of their own rights by individuals not only qua subjects of the state but also qua patients of instititutions such as medical institutions, started a story of contentious jurisdiction between citizens and institutions. All this, toward the end of the sixties, made the insulation of the academic Ivory Tower less and less waterproof, while at the same time internal change in academic philosophy had been marked enough as to allow for some reaction to demand coming from the outside world. Had such change been lacking, as it was in the case of countries such as France and Italy where ethics qua academic discipline was moribund the denouement would have been different, answers would have been provided more through legislation than by 'deciding together,' philosophers would have become even more isolated or on the contrary some of them would have tried to become gurus or political agitators – precisely what happened in France and Italy. For a number of reasons, the available intellectual supply met the new demand. This happened in the Anglo-Saxon world first, and then in a few Northern-European countries and Germany, and slightly after, dragged by the post-Franquist wind of change also in Spain.[73] So it happened that between 1903 and 1958 Anglo-Saxon philosophers used to quote the first three chapters of Moore's *Principia* and from 1958 started quoting the following chapters, or that Adorno used to quote Marx, Freud and Nietzsche, and his pupil Habermas started quoting Kant and Grotius and Pufendorf.

Alan Donagan aptly described the social context within which the normative turn took place in the Anglo-Saxon countries. He wrote:

> Until the 1960s, overt conflicts in Anglo-American society were social and political rather than moral: both those who suffered hostile discrimination and those who practised it, both liberals and conservatives, at least affected to believe that their opponents respected the same moral standards... In the 1960s, this ceased to be the case. First of all, black Americans, no longer content to criticize customs and laws that denied their human rights, refused to comply with them and denounced those who urged delay and caution. A little later, when Americans of all classes and races were liable to be drafted to fight in a war in Vietnam that few of them understood and that many who did considered to be morally wrong, the theory of just war, largely created

by medieval and counter-Reformation Catholics, began to supplant post-Kantian "Machiavellian" doctrines of the right of states to compel citizens to serve in wars they disapproved... in Britain... in 1956 G.E.M. Anscombe had provoked discussion of the then neglected classical theory of the just war by issuing a pamphlet opposing Oxford's conferring of an honorary degree on President Truman... Traditionally minded Catholics rightly foresaw that some views they cherished would be subverted by secular ideas; but, as the 1980s was to show, there would be reverse subversion.[74]

Onora O'Neill described the same change in the atmosphere breathed by moral philosophers in the seventies and eighties of the twentieth century in the following terms:

> Many point to the vivid contrast between the abstract and unpolitical character of ethical writing in the English-speaking world in the decade from G.E. Moore's *Principia Ethica* until John Rawls' *A Theory of Justice* (1971). In his period ethical writing was often preoccupied with the vicissitudes of personal life; in the past 15 years there had been much substantive, detailed and socially aware writing on problems of the public domain. These changes suggest that the positivist challenge to meaningful ethical discourse has finally been repulsed and that elaborated ethical theories and substantive arguments about handling specific cases can be introduced into the political arena.[75]

A Few Intermediate Considerations

Let me advance a few intermediate considerations.

a) There is still an old myth around the "death of ethics" in the beginning of the twentieth century. The myth is still lingering around, perhaps more in peripheral areas such as France and Italy, among other things because there is a grain of truth in it. In the culture of Continental Europe immoralism has been a comparatively popular attitude and in the British culture the character of Sidgwick's rational egoist has played a rôle not too far from that of the immoralist. What needs be amended is perhaps not the very idea of a death of ethics, but the idea of a *twentieth-century* death of ethics as a kind of end of a parable, the final point of the trajectory of modernity, and accordingly an unavoidable outcome of a logico-chronological unfolding. On the contrary, immoralism and ethical egoism are nothing new, surely not a *dernier cri*, but a strange persistence of an old/modern doctrine, namely Renaissance ethical scepticism.

b) A more interesting diagnosis is Apel's view of a complementarity between existentialist and scientistic forms of decisionism. According to Apel science was for both alignments the domain of facts without values while ethics was the domain of values without facts, and the two camps differed as to what factor should be given priority: either science as the one available basis of human coexistence or science and pure technology, apt top design power plants (this is Heidegger's image). Pragmatism, and other trends in the Anglo-Saxon as well as in the Continental world are a challenge to his diagnosis.

c) According to a famous witty remark by Donagan, Kant's was till a few years ago the moral philosophy almost nobody knows.[76] This wisecrack contained a grain of truth, since even a serious Kant scholar such as Ross moved to Kantian ethics what were after all unfair criticisms. Yet, this is no longer true after the Kantian renaissance of the nineties, and the best scholarship on Kant in the last few years has been coming from America. What is still true instead is that the moral philosophy nobody knows on the Continent is intuitionism, a strange doctrine about which Continental philosophers, and neo-analytic philosophers from the Continent, have heard something only from its enemies. This is important in order to account for the mistaken image of analytic ethics that European philosophers have shared until now, an image that has privileged either non-cognitivism or utilitarianism, missing the role played by the legacy of the controversy between intuitionism and utilitarianism and the obvious circumstance that half of twentieth-century analytic ethics, from Moore to Rawls through Ross and Prichard, was a form of weakened (and, as I have argued, vulnerable) intuitionism.

d) A related point is the enormous weight of the topic of moral dilemmas in both Anglo-Saxon and Continental ethics. In analytic ethics moral dilemmas are a legacy of Mill's and Sidgwick's controversy with classical intuitionism. Their main point was trying to prove that traditional moral systems (allegedly identified with intuitionism) were unable to carry out their own task since they carried unavoidable moral dilemmas. The notion of *prima facie* duty was a result of this controversy, and is based on assumptions that have been never carefully scrutinized after the controversy. For reasons still to be explored in depth (but I venture to say that they may be traced to Jesuitic probabilism and the Jansenists' attack on the Jesuits, via Pascal, Rousseau and Romanticism) the same topic has been central for the Continental existentialists. The outcome in their case was not prima face duties but the arbitrariness and uniqueness of decision.

e) Searle suggested a few years ago that analytic philosophy started with Hume and ended up with Kant. Analytic ethics probably followed the same trajectory as analytic epistemology, toward the discovery of constraints derived not from consequences or external sanctions but from the very activity of the law-governing subject. The reasons for this development need still to be questioned and may be of various kinds: internal reasons deriving from the course taken by the argument, demands posed by the growing number of problems of applied ethics and the apparent intractability within the framework of ruling ethical theories, external or semi-sociological reasons.

f) Continental philosophy in the first half of the century was, according to Apel's diagnosis, under the sway of Existentialism. A more careful diagnosis would be that also in the first half of the century there was a markedly rationalistic and normative Continental tradition, phenomenology, and that in its best expressions this tradition formulated several of the themes of the Anglo-Saxon rediscovery of normative ethics. The most popular trend of phenomenological ethics yet turned it into edifying discourse that invited deserved attacks, if not those of Heidegger and Sartre at least those of Adorno. After that, in the last three decades of the century, the most creative thinkers were either Kantians or

Aristotelians or some blend of the two things, and they were attentive to Anglo-Saxon traditions, in the best cases – those of Apel and Habermas – not just unimaginative import dealers introducing the last fashion from the centre of the Empire but rather discoverers of Anglo-Saxon trends that were comparatively forgotten by Anglo-Saxons themselves.

Notes

[1] See Stuart Hamspshire, "Fallacies in Moral Philosophy" [1949] in Id., *Freedom of Mind* (Oxford: Clarendon Press, 1972), 42–62.

[2] Elisabeth Anscombe, "Modern Moral Philosophy" [1958] in Ead., *Ethics, Religion and Politics* (Oxford: Blackwell, 1981), 26–42.

[3] See Philippa Foot, "Moral Beliefs" [1958] in Ead., *Virtues and Vices* (Oxford: Clarendon, 2002), 110–131, particularly 124–125.

[4] See Philippa Foot, "Morality as a System of Hypothetical Imperatives" [1972] ibidem, 157–173, particularly 171.

[5] See Peter Geach, "Good and Evil" in *Analysis*, 17: 1 (1956), 33–42; cf. Id. *The Virtues* (Cambridge: Cambridge University Press, 1979).

[6] See Stephen Toulmin, *An Examination of the Place of Reason in Ethics* [1950] (Chicago, Ill: Open Court, 1986).

[7] Kurt Baier, *The Moral Point of View: a Rational Basis for Ethics* (Ithaca, NY: Cornell University Press, 1958), 309.

[8] Ibidem, 314.

[9] Clarence I. Lewis, *An Analysis of Knowledge and Valuation* (Lasalle, Ill: The Open Court, 1946), book III.

[10] Ibidem, 527.

[11] Clarence I. Lewis, *The Ground and Nature of Right* (New York: Columbia University Press, 1955), 97.

[12] Ibidem.

[13] Ibidem, 81–82.

[14] Clarence I. Lewis, *The Categorical Imperative* [1958] in Id., *Values and Imperatives* (Stanford, Ca: Stanford University Press, 1969), 197–198.

[15] See William D. Hudson (ed.), *The Is-Ought Question. A Collection of Papers on the Central Problem in Moral Philosophy* (London: Macmillan, 1969).

[16] Arthur N. Prior, "The Autonomy of Ethics" [1960] in Id., *Papers in Logic and Ethics*, ed. by Peter T. Geach and Anthony I.P. Kenny (London: Duckworth, 1976), 88–96; Max Black, "The Gap between 'Is' and 'Should'" [1964] in Hudson (ed.), *The Is-Ought Question*, 99–113.

[17] John Searle, "How to Derive 'Ought' from 'Is'" [1964] in *Speech Acts* (Cambridge: Cambridge University Press, 1969), 175–198 (ch. 8 includes a revised version of the original paper).

[18] See Hans-Georg Gadamer, *Wahreit und Methode* [1960] in *Gesammelte Werke* (Tübingen: Mohr, 1985–1995), vol. I, 312–316.

[19] Hans-Georg Gadamer, "Hermeneutics and Social Science" in *Cultural Hermeneutics*, 2: 2 (1975), 307–316, quote at 312.

[20] See Hans-Georg Gadamer, *Was ist Praxis. Die Bedingungen gesellschaftlicher Vernunft* [1974] in *Gesammelte Werke*, vol. IV, 218.

[21] Hans-Georg Gadamer, *Über die Möglichkeit einer philosophischen Ethik* [1963] in *Gesammelte Werke*, vol. IV, 175–188, particularly 177–181.

[22] Ibidem, see 182–188.

[23] This discussion is documented in a bulky anthology edited by Manfred Riedel, *Rehabilitierung der praktischen Philosophie*, 2 vols. (Fribourg-en-Brisgau: Rombach, 1972–74), a title which repeats an expression first used by Karl-Heinz Ilting, "Hegels Auseinandersetzung mit der Aristotelischen Politik," in *Philosophisches Jahrbuch*, 71: 1 (1963–64), 38–58.

[24] Joachim Ritter, *Metaphysik und Politik* (Frankfurt a.M.: Suhrkamp, 1969).

[25] Ottfried Höffe, *Praktische Philosophie. Das Modell des Aristoteles* (München: Pustet, 1971).

[26] Robert Spaemann, *Moralische Grundbegriffe* (München: Beck, 1986).

[27] Rudiger Bubner, *Geschichtsprozesse und Handlungsnormen* (Frankfurt a.M.: Suhrkamp, 1984); Id., *Handlung, Sprache und Vernunft* (Frankfurt a.M.: Suhrkamp, 1976).

[28] Manfred Riedel, *Metaphysik und Metapolitik* (Frankfurt a.M.: Suhrkamp, 1975).

[29] Karl-Otto Apel, *Das Apriori der Kommunikationsgemeinschaft und die Grudlagen der Ethik* in Id., *Transformation der Philosophie*, 2 vols. (Frankfurt a.m.: Suhrkamp, 1973), 358–435, particularly 363–370; Ian Rohls, *Geschichte der Ethik* (Tübingen: Mohr, 1991), 443–451.

[30] Jürgen Habermas, *Theorie des kommunikativen Handeln*, 2 vols. (Frankfurt a.M.: Suhrkamp, 1981); Engl. transl. *The Theory of Communicative Action* (Boston: Beacon Press, 1985), ch. 5.

[31] Jürgen Habermas, "Sprachspiel, Intention und Bedeutung. Zu Motiven bei Sellars und Wittgenstein" in *Sprachanalyse und Soziologie*, ed. by Rolf Wiggershaus (Frankfurt a.M.: Suhrkamp, 1975), 319–340.

[32] See Jürgen Habermas, "Wahrheitstheorien" [1972] in Id., *Vorstudien und Ergänzungen zur Theorie des kommunikativen Handelns* (Frankfurt a.M.: Suhrkamp, 1984), 127–183, particularly 174–183; cf. Id., *Moralbewusstsein und kommunikatives Handeln* (Frankfurt a.M.: Suhrkamp, 1983); Engl. transl. *Moral Consciousness and Communicative Action*, ed. by Thomas McCarthy (Cambridge: Polity Press, 1990).

[33] Roy F. Harrod, "Utilitarianism Revised" in *Mind*, 45: 178 (1936), 137–156.

[34] The term appears in Richard B. Brandt, *Ethical Theory* (Englewood Cliffs, NJ: Prentice Hall, 1959).

[35] J. Harrison, "Utilitarianism, Universalization, and Our Duty to Be Just" in *Proceeding of the Aristotelian Society. New Series*, 53 (1952–1953), 105–134; James O. Urmson, "The Interpretation of the Moral Philosophy of J.S. Mill" in *The Philosophical Quarterly*, 3: 10 (1953), 33–39; Stephen Toulmin, *The Place of Reason in Ethics* [1950] (Chicago, Ill: Open Court, 1986); John Rawls, "Two Concepts of a Rule" in *The Philosophical Review*, 64: 1 (1955), 3–32.

[36] David Lyons, *Forms and Limits of Utilitarianism* (Oxford: Clarendon Press, 1965).

[37] See Richard M. Hare, *Moral Thinking* (Oxford: Clarendon Press, 1981).

[38] See Id., *Sorting out Ethics* (Oxford: Clarendon Press, 1997), ch. VIII.

[39] See Richard B. Brandt, *A Theory of the Good and the Right* (Oxford: Clarendon Press, 1979).

[40] See Id., *Hopi Ethics: a Theoretical Analysis* (Chicago, Ill: University of Chicago Press, 1954).

[41] See Id., *A Theory of the Good and the Right*, 196–199; Id., *Morality, Utilitarianism, and Rights* (Cambridge: Cambridge University Press, 1992), 299.

[42] See John C. Harsanyi, "Morality and the Theory of Rational Behavior" [1977] in *Utilitarianism and Beyond*, ed. by Amartya Sen and Bernard Williams (Cambridge: Cambridge University Press, 1982), 39–62; Id., "Advances in Understanding Rational Behavior" in Id., *Essays on Ethics, Social Behavior, and Scientific Explanation* (Dordrecht: Reidel, 1976), 89–117; Id., "Ethics in Terms of Hypothetical Imperatives" [1958] ibidem, 24–36.

[43] Peter Singer, *Practical Ethics* (Cambridge: Cambridge University Press, 1997); Id., *Rethinking Life and Death. The Collapse of our Traditional Ethics* (New York: St Martin's Press, 1994); Id., *Writings on an Ethical Life* (New York: Ecco Press, 2001); Helga Kuhse, *The Sanctity-of-Life Doctrine in Medicine: a Critique* (Oxford: Clarendon, 1987); James Rachels, *The End of Life* (Oxford: Oxford University Press, 1986).

[44] Peter Singer, *Practical Ethics*, ch. 1.

[45] Sørensen A., *Deontology – Born and Kept in Servitude by Utilitarianism*, forthcoming.

[46] John Rawls, *A Theory of Justice* (Cambridge, Mass: Harvard University Press, 1971), 251–257.

[47] John Rawls, "Kantian Constructivism in Moral Theory," in *The Journal of Philosophy*, 77: 9 (1980), 515–572.

[48] John Rawls, *Political Liberalism* (Cambridge, Mass: Harvard University Press, 1993), lecture II, note 7.

[49] See Robert Nozick, *Anarchy, State and Utopia* (New York: Basic Books 1974); Id. *Philosophical Explanations* (Cambridge, Mass: Harvard University Press, 1981), part V; Ronald M. Dworkin, *Taking Rights Seriously* (London: Duckworth, 1977); *Freedom's Law; The Moral Reading of the American Constitution* (Cambridge, Mass: Harvard University Press, 1999); Alan Gewirth, *Human Rights: Essays on Justification and Applications*, (Chicago, Ill: University of Chicago Press, 1982); Id., *The Community of Rights* (Chicago, Ill: University of Chicago Press, 1996).

[50] Alan Gewirth, *Reason and Morality* (Chicago, Ill: University of Chicago Press, 1978); Id., "The Future of Ethics. The Moral Powers of Reason" in *Nous* 15: 1 (1981), 15–30.

[51] See Albrecht Wellmer, *Ethik und Dialog* (Frankfurt a.M.: Suhrkamp, 1986); Eng. Transl. *Ethics and Dialogue: Elements of Moral Judgement in Kant and Discourse Ethics*, in Id., *The Persistence of Modernity* (Oxford: Polity Press, 1991); Jürgen Habermas, *Faktizität und Geltung* (Frankfurt a.M.: Suhrkamp, 1992); Eng. transl. *Between facts and Norms*, (Cambridge, Mass: MIT Press, 1996).

[52] See Alan Donagan, "Philosophical Ethics: what it is and what it should be" in *The Philosophical Papers*, 2 vols., ed. by J.E. Malpas (Chicago, Ill: The University of Chicago Press, 1994), vol. II, 262–282.

[53] See Antonin-Dalmace Sertillanges, *La pensée morale de Saint Thomas d'Aquin* [1916] (Paris : Aubier-Montaigne, 1961); Wolfgang Kluxen, *Philosophische Ethik bei Thomas von Aquin* (Mainz: Grünewald, 1964).

[54] See John Finnis, *Moral Absolutes: Tradition, Revision, and Truth* (Washington DC: Catholic University of America Press, 1991).

[55] The most respectable example of such rule-utilitarian 'foundation' of ethics is still the one provided by Richard B. Brandt, *A Theory of the Good and the Right* (Oxford: Clarendon Press, 1979), ch. 6.

[56] See Sergio Cremaschi, *The Mill-Wheell Controversy on Ehics and its Bequest to Analytic Philosophy*, *Rationality in Belief and Action*, ed. by Elvio Baccarini and Snežana Prijiæ Samaržja (Rijeka: University of Rijeka: Faculty of Arts and Sciences – Croatian Society for Analytic Philosophy, 2006), 45–62.

[57] Richard M. Hare, *Moral Thinking* (Oxford: Clarendon Press, 1981), ch. 2, § 5.

[58] See for example Mark Timmons, *Morality without Foundations: a Defense of Ethical Contextualism* (New York: Oxford University Press, 1999).

[59] 'Moral particularism' has been the flag under which the new trend of post-neo-intuitionists, led perhaps by Jonathan Dancy, has marched; the trend basically argues a return to David Ross while getting rid of his lists of prima facie principles, on the basis of their uselessness once judgment engages in valuing concrete cases. See *Moral Particularism* ed. by Brad Hooker and Margaret O. Little (Oxford: Oxford University Press, 2000).

[60] See Alan Donagan, "Is there a Credible Form of Utilitarianism?" in *The Philosophical Papers of Alan Donagan*, 2 vols., ed. by Jeff E. Malpas, (Chicago: The University of Chicago Press, 1994), vol. II, 132–143.

[61] William Paley, *The Principles of Moral and Political Philosophy* [1785], ed. by Dan L. LeMahieu (Indianapolis, Ind: Liberty Fund, 2002), book II, ch. 6.

[62] See John Rawls, *A Theory of Justice* (Cambridge, Mass: Harvard University Press, 1971), 30.

[63] See Hare, *Moral Thinking*, ch. 9.

[64] See for example, Roberto M. Unger, *Knowledge and Politics* (New York: The Free Press, 1976), 59–62.

[65] See Bernard Williams, *Ethics and the Limits of Philosophy* (Cambridge: Cambridge University Press, 1985), ch. 10; Michael Stocker, "The Schizophrenia of Modern Ethical Theories" in *Journal of Philosophy*, 73: 14 (1976), 453–466; Alasdair MacIntyre, *After Virtue* (Notre Dame, In: University of Notre Dame Press, 1981), ch. 14.

[66] See Sergio Cremaschi, "L'etica delle virtù: commenti a Berti" in *Etica e Politica/ Ethics & Politics*, 4: 2 (2005), 1–13.

[67] See Martha Nussbaum, "Virtue Ethics, a Misleading Category?" *The Journal of Ethics*, 3: 1 (1999), 163–301.

[68] See Alasdair MacIntyre, *Dependent Rational Animals* (Notre Dame, Ind: Notre Dame University Press, 1999); Martha Nussbaum, "Nature, Function and Capability" in *Oxford Studies in Ancient Philosophy*, Supplementary volume I (1988), 145–184; Ead., "Non-relative Virtues" in *The Quality of Life* (Oxford: Clarendon Press, 1991), 242–276.

[69] Bernard Williams, *Ethics and the Limits of Philosophy* (Cambridge: Cambridge University Press, 1985).

[70] Onora O'Neill, *Towards Justice and Virtue* (Cambridge: Cambridge University Press, 1996).

[71] Christine M. Koorsgard et al., *The Sources of Normativity*, ed. by Onora O'Neill (Cambridge: Cambridge University Press, 2000); Nancy Sherman, "The Place of Emotions in Kantian Morality" in *Identity, Character and Morality*, ed. by Amelie Rorty, Owen Flanagan (Cambridge, Mass: MIT Press, 1990), 149–170; Ead., *Making a Necessity of Virtue* (Cambridge: Cambridge University Press, 1997); Barbara Herman, *The Practice of Moral Judgement* (Cambridge, Mass: Harvard University Press 1993); Marcia Baron, *A Kantian Ethics Almost Without Apology* (Ithaca, NY: Cornell University Press, 1995).

[72] See Stephen Darwall, *Impartial Reasons* (Ithaca: Cornell University Press, 1983).

[73] For English readers at least two books by the spiritual father of the new Spanish practical philosophy is now available: see: Javier Muguerza, *Ethics and Perplexity. Toward a Critique of Dialogical Reason*, ed. by John R. Welch (Amsterdam: Rodopi, 2004) and *The Alternative of Dissent* (Cambridge: Cambridge University Press, 1989).

[74] Alan Donagan, "History of Western Ethics: 12. twentieth-century Anglo-American" in *Encyclopedia of Ethics. Second Edition*, ed. by Lawrence C. Becker and Charlotte B. Becker, 3 vols. (New York: Routledge, 2001), vol. II, 769.

[75] Onora O'Neill, *Faces of Hunger. An Essay on Poverty, Justice and Development* (London: Allen & Unwin, 1986).

[76] Alan Donagan, "The Moral Theory Almost Nobody Knows: Kant's" in *The Philosophical Papers of Alan Donagan*, vol. ii, 44–152.

CHAPTER 3

The Applied Ethics Revolution

Conscientious Objectors and Ethical Committees

Applied ethics, according to an authoritative definition, is "distinguished commonly as that part of ethics that gives particular and direct attention to practical issues and controversies."[1] According to another, it is

> the application of ethical considerations – reasons, principles, values, ideals – to any policy or practice – personal or social – for the purpose of evaluating (and thus endorsing or rejecting) the policy or practice on ethical grounds. Thus, applied ethics is the branch of practical reasoning in which ethical (as opposed to prudential or selfish) considerations are employed to guide individual and collective conduct.[2]

The birth of applied ethics cannot be neatly located some time *after* my preferred date for the normative turn, 1958, since its birth-date is 1956, the year when Elisabeth Anscombe, one of the key figures in the normative turn plot, before liquidating the whole modern moral philosophy business in twenty pages, published a pamphlet where she attacked Oxford University's honorary degree to Harry Truman on the basis of Scholastic just war theory. Her argument was that the President of the United States was a war criminal for having bombed civilian targets with no strictly military goal towards the end of the war with Japan,[3] which amounted to referring to Francisco de Vitoria, the main authority in Scholastic just war theory who declared that "*Numquam licet per se et ex intentione interficere innocentem.*"[4]

But it is actually around 1971 that the real boom took place. This was the year of John Rawls's *A Theory of Justice*, and the year in which Van

71

Raenseler Potter introduced the very term bioethics, followed a year later by Richard Hare's *Applications of Moral Philosophy* and his pupil Peter Singer's paper "Famine, Affluence, and Morality."[5] The birth of bioethics, now 'normalized' into an academic sub-discipline insulated enough in order to avoid too much trouble to what was going on elsewhere, was cause and effect of a culture shock, no less disquieting than those related to Feminism and Pacifism, the discovery that what had been going on as obvious in hospitals and laboratories was far from obvious, and indeed concealed a number of horrible practices, or at least of practices deeply at variance with the principles of a democratic society, that ceased to be democratic as soon as one ceased being a citizen and became a patient. Albert R. Jonsen, the father of one of the approaches in bioethics, aptly describes the climate of the years in which bioethics was brought to life. He writes:

My autobiography, like those of my colleagues, reveals in a personal way how bio-ethics came to be. During my graduate studies and my tenure at USF, very real ethical problems were agitating the national conscience. Persons who chose to study academic ethics, philosophical or religious, could not immure themselves within classical treatises, The Civil Rights movement stirred passions… Sentiment against the war in Southeast Asia grew during the late sixties and had reached fever pitch by the time I was professor at USF. Many of my students sought my advice about conscientious objection to military service. This was a peculiarly difficult problem for Catholics, Roma Catholic theology taught a doctrine of "just war": warfare was ethically justified under certain conditions. American courts had recognized conscientious objection only for the traditional "peace churches," such as the Quakers and the Mennonites, which repudiated all warfare, I served as a confessor and advisor to many of these perplexed young Catholics. I knew how complex the moral issue was because my graduate student colleague, Jim Childress, had written a brilliant dissertation on conscientious objection. My uncle, Federal Judge William T. Sweigert, was among the first to declare the war unconstitutional.

So, during my first year as a student and teacher of ethics, I became deeply and personally engaged in very real ethical issues.[6]

The Methods of Applied Ethics

Of the early history of bioethics the most striking feature is the discovery of a plurality of 'Methods.' Here methods means precisely what Sidgwick had in mind when he wrote *The Methods of Ethics*, that is, a procedure by which normative conclusions may be reached on a given moral case. It is worth recalling that for Sidgwick such a search for method ends in "unavoidable failure." On the contrary developments in bioethics have shown how more than one procedure is available.

Consequentialism, as Anscombe had re-dubbed the old doctrine of utilitarianism, was apparently the ruling doctrine during the first phase of the history of bioethics. For consequentialists such as Peter Singer, Helga Kuhse and James Rachels, bioethics is a matter of minimising suffering, and its raison-d'être was the coming of a widespread secularised mental attitude for which the old morality was prejudice and superstition, best described as the paradigm of the sacrality of life, that is taboo or magic thinking. The one self-evident standard for such a mentality is the quality, not the sacrality of life, the one method for justified choices is calculation of consequences, the morally relevant distinctions are those between the quality of the life of sentient beings; all the rest is "sacrality of life" and accordingly nonsense.

Consequentialism produced its own where in a first phase strange bed-fellows were grouped together under the label of "deontology," a label that was invented by the consequentialists themselves. This highly artificial cluster included – according to its consequentialist critics – Kantians and intuitionists together with Thomists and Aristotelians and theologians of any description, under the assumption that all these were traditional or old moral doctrines, basically to be identified with divine command theories, that are the best expression of the old paradigm of the sacrality of life. In case Aquinas happens to declare that the moral law is not

73

the result of God's will but of his intellect or Kant declare that it is not biological life that is sacred but persons as subjects of free choice and moral responsibility that deserve infinite respect, the strategy adopted by the proponents of the new morality has constantly been ignoring what the opponent was saying.

While utilitarianism was the most popular doctrine during the first phase of bioethics, only a limited number of voices in this field argued some kind of 'deontological' approach. Among then was Edmund Pellegrino who proposed a revision of the Hyppocratic tradition in the light of new scientific and technical developments and the new awareness of the patient's rights and autonomy,[7] and Robert Veatch who proposed a revision of traditional medical ethics on a contractarian basis aimed at defining a physician-patient relationship as a relationship between equals.[8] From the eighties bioethicists with Kantian or right-based leanings tended to align themselves with the first of the new 'mixed theory,' the principles approach. The theory was presented in 1979 by Tom L. Beauchamp and James F. Childress in their *Principles of Medical Ethics.*[9] They started with an 'empirical' discovery, namely the fact that the members of the National Commission for the Protection of Human Subjects of Biomedical and Behavioral Research that yielded the well-known Belmont Report of 1978[10] had reached an agreement on a number of 'intermediate' principles, while starting each from his own religious and philosophical outlook, and without reaching any agreement on 'ultimate' principles. A lesson they drew from the Belmont Report is that there is a way for reaching partial agreements on controversial moral issues even between upholders of opposed comprehensive ethical theories. One consequence is that such theories need not be fully developed before trying to settle dilemmas in applied ethics, and another is that the existence of alternative comprehensive views is no insurmountable cause of dissent on collective choices. The way out of disagreement is application to the individual case of 'intermediate' principles about which – as John Stuart Mill had already remarked – agreement is reached more easily than about ultimate principles. In real-world issues an agreement about the principles, even without any agreement on the principle's foundation, may be enough in order to work out shared policies. Beauchamp and Childress's principles are four intermediate principles they believe are shared by both Utilitarians and 'Deontologists': a) respect for autonomy; b) non-maleficence; c) beneficence; d) equity or justice. They are understood as *prima facie* principles, in David Ross's sense, and the task of bioethics is applying them to concrete cases by adopting two strategies: a) specification; b) balancing. Moral knowledge – they insist much in a Rossian mood – is reached in a way not dependent on any essential order of "inference or dependence"[11] and the relationship between principles and cases echoes the idea of reflective equilibrium that had been proposed (or better, transposed to ethics from philosophy of science, where it had been introduced by Nelson Goodman) by John Rawls: principles need to be made case-specific, and the analysis of cases needs to be enlightened by general principles. In turn – it may be noted – Rawls took advantage of Beauchamp and Childress's approach in the version of his own theory, in so far as his 'overlapping consensus' is precisely a kind of agreement on a principle between parts adopting different foundations for the principle. A few comments are in order. The first is that that principle was a revival of early twentieth-century neo-intuitionism of a Ross-kind, no less than John Rawls theory was. The second is that it was a bland version of a 'traditional' and 'deontological' normative ethics. The third, and the one on which most critics concentrated, is that the idea of "autonomy" or "respect for autonomy" is far from innocent: either it is a full-blown Kantian idea, with the costs to be paid for adoption of so marked an idea, or it tends to boil down to a typically American individualist myth, a blend of Lockean and Millian ideas.

The new casuistry or the cases approach was the second mixed method proposed for bioethics as a way of solving the same problem, that is finding a solution for real cases while facing enduring dissent on principles. It was proposed by Albert Jonsen and Stephen Toulmin[12] nine years after Beauchamp and Childress's book, as something that was already out there as a practice followed by ethical committees no less than the practice of finding an agreement on intermediate principles. It consists basically in the same kind of procedures as Beauchamp and Childress's but with an alleged advantage, namely the fact of paying a lesser toll on the way to agreement. The intersection in the cases approach in fact is not a principle, but just a paradigmatic case, about which there is already a shared conclusion. And the process then is not top-down, or deductive, as for the former approach, but instead analogical, inductive, 'abductive' (in Peirce's sense), or 'topical' (in the sense of ancient rhetoric). Jonsen, who was a Jesuit and had first-hand knowledge of the tradition of sixteenth-century casuistry, highlighted how this approach, rediscovered inductively in the medical practice is basically the method of the old casuistry, which had been unfairly denigrated by almost all modern moral philosophers who followed blindly Blaise Pascal's misrepresentation of casuistry that identified it as such with the claims of one particular current, laxism. The strength of casuistry lies, according to Jonsen and Toulmin, in its ability to content itself with a shared conclusion on a case accepted as paradigmatic as a starting-point for our quest for shared judgments on new cases. Casuistic analysis of moral cases works with paradigms and analogies aiming at an informed opinion on the existence and the degree of strength of particular moral obligations, expressed by rules and maxims that are general albeit not universal or unchanging, since they hold in the conditions specific to one given agent and set of circumstances, and the solution for the individual case depends on a judgement that is 'prudential' in its character, or resting on Aristotelian *phronesis*.[13] The comments are in order that the new casuistry is a kind of coherentist, non-foundationalist approach to moral argument; that it is an approach not absolutely different from principlism, but basically the same kind of approach working with less assumptions; that, ironically, it is a revival of the 'old' morality *par excellence*, that is, of the morality once taught in theological faculties and mocked by Sidgwick.

Both mixed approaches were soon attacked by an assorted company of 'alternative' approaches who shared only one point, namely disdain of theory as too abstract. The first 'third way' between consequentialism and deontology, namely virtue ethics, yielded also a number of alternative approaches to bioethics. Among the first to try such an approach was Daniel Callahan who, like MacIntyre and others, combined virtue ethics with communitarianism. From such a viewpoint he intended to unveil unacknowledged individualist assumptions in the discussion of central issues in bioethics. For example, discussion about euthanasia was biased by the hidden assumption that it is a matter of course that if anybody wants something that medicine is able to offer he has right to it, unless it may be proved that this would imply damage to a third part,[14] and such assumptions tend to deny the relational character of our existence where, instead, being born and dying are events concerning not only individuals but subjects who belong to a network of relationships.[15] After 'pure' virtue ethics there was the care approach, whose founder was Carol Gilligan as well as other feminist approaches, proposed by Susan Sherwin, Susan Wolf and others who have emphasized wider dimensions of moral deliberation in concrete situations and have argued some masculine character of deontological and consequentalist theories.[16] As a whole, a number of approaches, including the care approach, the anti-theory movement, and most of feminist ethics are variously related with, and point at basically the same direction as the composed phenomenon that has been named virtue ethics. The main points stressed have been: a) there are more dimensions of action than conformity to duty; b) emotions matter; c) the individual as such is a myth, since the original datum is individuals in a network of relationships; d) uncertainty in the individual case is such as to make moral theories, qua theories, irrelevant and ineffective.

After classical theories, mixed theories, anti-theory approaches, the fourth 'method' of bioethics is provided by the family of the 'deliberative' approaches. These have emphasized the idea that, and applied ethics and bioethics as a case thereof, are not specifications of some ethical doctrine, but instead a kind of real-world process of *deliberation* (different from *bargaining, majority rule* and even contractarian procedures) assisted by 'technicians of reason' in order to reach agreement on practical decisions in a way that may take into account different reasons to which different partners are committed and yet may yield a virtuous compromise, whence all partners come out with no loss and some gain. Among the proponents of such approaches are neo-Aristotelians, and obviously enough Hans-Georg Gadamer was the first of them, neo-pragmatists, and Kantians, among whom the most consequent theorist of deliberation was Onora O'Neill.[17] Also among supporters of deliberations, some have pointed too at real-world examples of their preferred procedures that have antedated their own theories. One was the example of Oregon, where in the early 80s an extended debate involving thousands of citizens was carried out in organized discussion groups assisted by specialists who offered detailed information on various aspects of alternative policies under examination with a view to working out guidelines for health policies.

> This project – one warm sympathiser of such procedures comments – falls into a tradition in recent liberal political philosophy that can be associated with John Dewey. Dewey was strongly influenced by town meeting democracy… Community consultation is arguably a requirement of liberal democracy, so that members of the polity have the opportunity to express themselves on substantive moral questions, the answers to which are certain to affect them.[18]

A less known example of the same kind of virtuous compromise was the Italian law on abortion passed in the late seventies by a majority in Parliament that was not coincident with the one supporting the government in charge, and was not precisely described in terms of left against right. It was written after an extended discussion in the 'civil society' where on the one hand the voice was heard of women's movements who tended to frame the issue in terms different from the individualist terms of individual rights in which the extreme liberal-individualist *Partito Radicale* had first framed the issue, and on the other a liberal current of Catholic intellectuals and politicians, whose senator Raniero La Valle was the most influential voice, gave a contribution to the discussion of policies for prevention of recourse to abortion as one side of an overall policy on the issue, where self-determination by women was the other. Partial convergences were reached in Parliament notwithstanding disagreement on the morality of abortion as such and possibly as a final result of such a virtuous compromise strategy, in 1982 a referendum promoted by pro-life organizations with heavy involvement of the Catholic-Church establishment against the bill passed by Parliament, scored much less (30%) than a previous one, in 1974, for abolishing divorce (40%), which was obviously enough a less dramatic moral issue. Apparently either ten percent of the public opinion had become less conservative and less prone to directions by the bishops in only eight years, or a significant part of possible opponents to abortion was convinced enough that the 'virtuous' compromise reached was at least a lesser evil for disregarding the bishops' directions.

The New Political Philosophy qua Applied Ethics

In the years of the birth of bioethics, a parallel phenomenon was the birth of the new political philosophy that was basically 'normative analysis.' In the first half of the century political philosophy consisted either of political realism or of linguistic analysis of the language of politics, with a neo-Aristotelian enclave identified with Leo Strauss's school. The turn started by Rawls between the fifties and the sixties consisted in treating the issues of political philosophy by means of a revised form of intuitionism (the then most execrated form of normative ethics in the Anglo-Saxon word) where the cognitive claims of intuitions are weakened to a maximum and the coherentist potential of the intuitionist approach is stressed as much as possible. So, Rawls's first theory as it was presented in 1971 in *A Theory of Justice*[19] was meant as a grammar of 'our' sense of justice, as it is de facto shared by us as citizens of a liberal-democratic society, and its strategy was that of adjusting or rectifying our judgments on novel or controversial issues starting with more familiar cases where there is an established consensus.

These were comparatively strange ideas, and were rather overlooked in a first phase by the readers of Rawls, most of all by those in Europe who ignored his background in Anglo-Saxon twentieth-century ethics and read him through the glasses they were familiar with – Hobbes, Locke and Rousseau – and accordingly took him as a neo-contractualist. In fact Rawls's 'official' program was a revival of seventeenth-century political contractualism, his hidden agenda was a revival of anti-utilitarian ethics through the elaboration of a weakened version of intuitionism. He took from the neo-intuitionist Harold Prichard the idea of a priority of the right over the good, from the proponent of the good reasons approach Kurt Baier the idea of a procedural justification of the adoption of a system of rules, from the philosopher of science Nelson Goodman the idea of 'reflexive equilibrium.'[20] His concern in the fifties was to find a way out of a stalemate in ethics, resulting from prevailing interest for metaethics which in turn yielded a kind of inconclusive debate that had nothing to say on normative ethics and which, for this reason, used to leave the latter field to the few surviving proponents of utilitarianism. The way out he believed he had found resulted from turning the familiar terms of the relationship between metaethics and normative ethics upside down. He set forth as a first step the formulation of a satisfactory normative ethics and then, as a consequence, clarification of issues in metaethics. He believed that twentieth-century metaethical inquiry had gone astray for the reason that, as in the philosophy of mathematics, also in the philosophy of morality there are serious limits to what conceptual and linguistic analysis can do.[21] A theory of justice is not conceptual and linguistic analysis but instead a true theory, subject to the same rules of method as other theories, and "definitions and analyses of meaning do not have a special place: definition is but one device used in setting up the general structure of theory,"[22] and it is accordingly "impossible to found a substantive theory of justice on the sole basis of definitions and logical truths."[23] Moral philosophy should be – as Aristotle and his followers up to Sidgwick used to think – "free to use at will contingent hypotheses and general facts as it pleases."[24] The raw materials of "moral theory" is our "sense of justice," that is our capacity of "judging things to be just and unjust"[25] and motivating our judgments. Moral philosophy is an attempt at *describing* our moral capacity, not a "list of the judgments on institutions and actions that we are prepared to render, accompanied with supporting reasons when these are offered,"[26] but instead the construction of a set of principles that, facing analogous circumstances, would lead us to formulate such judgments. Rawls draws a parallel with Noam Chomsky's linguistic theory that makes room for a "deep grammar" opposed to ordinary grammar,[27] and suggests that moral theory does something similar to what grammar does, that is defining the capacity of recognizing well-formed sentences by means of explicit principles that can perform the same distinctions the native speaker can perform. The criterion of truth to be adopted in moral theory is coherentist, as in linguistics and unlike physics, but nonetheless there is "a definite if limited class of facts against which conjectured principles can be checked, namely our considered judgements in reflective equilibrium."[28] Moral philosophy is different from that kind of objective knowledge which is instantiated by science; it is shaped by self-examination, it is "Socratic"[29] discourse, where all that one may reasonably ask of the theory is that it "seems on reflection to clarify and to order our thoughts"[30] and tend to reduce disagreements and bring divergent convictions more in line,"[31] that is a kind of discourse where we start with what "we" think, as David Ross claimed,[32] even if Ross's stronger intuitionist epistemological assumptions have been dropped.

What Rawls perhaps never fully realized is that dropping those assumptions turns his would-be "moral theory" into something more different from Ross's moral theory than he is prepared to admit. That

81

is, when read in the way I have tried to read it, Rawls' project looks rather similar to that of the new casuists, and it appears to be basically a coherentist strategy for treating moral disagreement with no claim at exploring foundational issues. This was not completely clear in 1971 when Rawls occasionally declared that his theory was also an application of rational choice theory (which it is not, as he admitted in 1993) and most of all a kind of new contractarian approach in the line of Hobbes, Locke etc. (which again it is not, since the contractarian procedure is avowedly only a didactic way of presenting the result of the reflexive or dialogical procedure through which normative conclusions are reached. Rawls's evolution between 1971 and 1993, when he published Political Liberalism,[33] parallels fairly well the direction of the evolution of applied ethics at large in the same years. The basic changes he introduced consisted in abandoning the ideal-contractarian procedure and the assumptions of rational choice in favour of real-world historically given kinds of agreement and of the idea of overlapping consensus. This is a contingent agreement between holders of different general worldviews who agree, each for his own reasons, on a moral basis for civil coexistence.

This evolution seems to make it clear, on the one hand, that philosophy in Rawls's hands collapses into American common sense but also, on the other, that Rawls towards the end of his career tends to put more into brackets the 'really' philosophical ethical doctrines such as utilitarianism and intuitionism, and points instead at working out procedures for establishing in a 'reasonable' way the basis for coexistence within historically given societies. This is perhaps no longer philosophy (much like casuistry did not claim to be philosophy) but it is perhaps just a fruitful way of accounting for processes of creation of liberal democratic institutions in ways not available to previous trends in political philosophy, that were undoubtedly more philosophical but also had nothing to say on such matters.

Thus, is political philosophy after Rawls just applied ethics? The answer is yes and no. No, insofar as theories stand in complex relationship to each other, and may be considered to be part of another for some aspect, and self-contained for other aspects. No, in case one adheres to political realism, which turns politics into something on principle independent of ethics. No, in case an ethical theory has such stringent requirements as to leave no room for agreement with those who have not been educated to the right philosophy, and the paramount example is Plato's *Republic*, which is, on this reason, ethics *applied*, but not applied ethics. The answer may be yes, and political philosophy may be seen as just one more field of applied ethics as far as it is normative discourse, and as far as its premises are assumed to result possibly from convergence among holders of different more general views.

A Slightly Odd Example: Development Ethics

After an obvious example, bioethics, and a rather controversial one, political philosophy, I will discuss a hitherto marginal case, development ethics, in order to show some recurrent patterns in the revival of the various (old and new) branches applied ethics.

A body of literature on related subjects grew during the last 30 years around an easily identifiable knot, the issue of underdevelopment. When such literature reached the required critical mass, the convention arose of describing it by the term "development ethics," the "normative or ethical discussion of ends and means of Third world development and global development."[34] Such literature, or the best of it, shares one basic trait of recent literature in bioethics and the new political theory, that is the strategy of immunizing dissent about basic issues and making rational argument possible among parts still dissenting about world-views, religions, full-blown philosophical views.

Denis Goulet, the putative father of the discipline, launched from the sixties the discussion on costs and perverse effects of well-meant development programs in terms of social relations, of culture, of subjective reactions by the concerned populations.[35] Peter Berger argued that the study of political ethics applied to social change is directly relevant to the discussion of Third World development.[36] A number of scholars from the third world contributed to the discussion from the very beginning,[37] and in 1984 the IDEA (International Development Ethics Association) was founded.[38]

Goulet suggests the names of Mohandas Karamchand Gandhi, Louis-Joseph Lebret and Gunnar Myrdal as forerunners of development ethics because of acknowledgement by all of them of the role of 'moral' factors in making the action of strictly economic factors possible:[39] after them, during the sixties, a discussion developed on the limits of a purely economic approach to development; a real act of birth of development ethics, or a threshold after which the discipline started autonomous life, was reached in the seventies, when a number of contributions by moral philosophers on poverty and underdevelopment appeared and everybody realized that the discussion could not go on among social scientists without bringing in philosophers. The definition now accepted seems to be that of a "normative or ethical discussion of means and ends of Third World development as well as global development."[40]

A parallel development has taken place in academic Anglo-Saxon philosophy where an interesting discussion of the duty to help the poor started in the early seventies. A now famous paper by Peter Singer started a discussion on the duty to give relief to people suffering from world-hunger, arguing that suffering and death by starvation are evil, and there is shared consensus on this point, albeit for possibly different reasons; it is our duty to make sure that nothing evil should happen even if we are not responsible for it, provided that we do not sacrifice to this end something with an equal moral relevance, and this point seems to be agreed upon to the same extent as the previous one; there are no plausible reasons for keeping the traditional distinction between duty and charity, as well as for taking proximity into account and for making a decisive difference between the case in which we are the only person who can avoid the evil under discussion and the one in which we are one among millions; we have to contribute as much as we can up to the point where we reduce ourselves to the level of marginal utility; the best way to contribute is by supporting organizations acting to spread birth control.[41] A remarkable trait of Singer's contribution is his starting from some widely accepted normative premise, that would do for Utilitarians as well as for followers of more traditional kinds of morality. This move – similar to others I have recalled as made by path-breakers in other fields of applied ethics – is more remarkable being made by somebody who was to become the leader of a markedly utilitarian approach in applied ethics.

A claim opposite to Singer's was advanced in another famous paper by Garrett Hardin[42] who proposed an analogy between developed countries and lifeboats, based on the existing limits in resources such as energy, environment, food, and room, as well as by paradoxes or tragedies carried by the existence of 'commons' (resources exploited by everybody but devoid of a superintendent authority with power to enforce limitations.[43] Hardin argues that there is a prudential duty as well as a responsibility to future generations that both recommend not to erode margins left in resources to richer nations; he argues that immediate relief is ineffective, that poor populations cannot advance a right to relief, that we lack criteria for allocating possible relief, and even more have no justified claim to the space and natural resources of richer nations such as the United States for reasons analogous to the legal ones regulating prescription as property rights are concerned.

The terms in which the discussion had been framed were drastically changed by Onora O'Neill who denied a number of assumptions shared by both Singer and Hardin. Her starting-point was that there is more to be allocated than just sums of money, or amounts of material commodities, and accordingly criteria for a just system of allocation have to be more complicated than those allowed for by Utilitarianism that make room just for a one-dimensional measurement of magnitudes of 'good.' That is, Singer's point may be made defensible against Hardin but only if we start with theoretical assumptions that are both less demanding and less 'queer' than those of a utilitarian theory and without losing in effectiveness even if formulating much less demanding prescriptions. Note that Neill also makes the same *epoché* or bracketing of the theoretical basis of her argument that Singer had done. She writes that

> the argument in this paper does not depend on any particular theory on the foundations of the obligation [of adoption a policy against hunger], but should be a corollary of any non-bizarre ethical theory that leave some room for the notion of rights.[44]

O'Neill's argument runs as follows. There are a few assumptions that could claim too to be widely shared ones, indeed to be more widely shared than Singer's, since they are more minimal. They are: a) people have a right not to be killed in an unjustified way (it is less than Singer's claim that people have a right not to be let die by those who could prevent it); b) a duty to defend others from being killed is not a wide duty of beneficence but a strict duty of enforcing other people's right not to be killed; c) the distinction between killing and letting die is not a distinction between *negative* and *positive* acts, but one based on the extent to which the individual act changes the existing state of affairs with a view to a person's survival; d) property rights do not override other people's right not to be killed.

Then there is a description of the state of affairs, which is different from Hardin's: a) the whole heart, (not an individual country) is a lifeboat; b) there are interdependencies by which hunger in underdeveloped countries is connected by causal chains with our actions.

The positive argument runs as follows: a) economic activities by some groups do cause the death of others; b) as individuals, even if we do not directly kill, yet we do kill and not only let die as a result of concomitant actions that do have causal influence; c) we have a duty to prevent deaths from hunger; d) policies may consist either of adopting specific policies that would head to less deaths (but this is undetermined unless the temporal horizon be specified), or in establishing the justification on which the right not to be killed might be subordinated to a competing right; e) the goal of anti-hunger policies is avoiding to kill those who are already born, not maximizing the population's average utility, or the question is not: how many can we add, but how few can we succeed in losing? f) anti-hunger policies may be soft or drastic population policies, or resources policies.

In *Faces of Hunger*[45] O'Neill added the following points: a) a Kantian ethics enjoys a few assets in assisting deliberation on issues connected with world-hunger, since it adopts an abstract (albeit not 'idealised') view of human agency that may be 'accessible' to agents with contrasting world-views; b) the duty to act non-unjustly starts with is universal and not related to particular roles; c) also the duty to respect and help developing talents is universal; d) such duties may be connected in actual deliberation with more specific grids used by different agents in different circumstances; e) Kantian justice may be enforced only through wide-scale political activities that transform basic principles of economic and social structures; f) a Kantian view of justice implies a revised 'moral point of view' where non-coercion and non-deception be made basic; g) instead of developing economic implications of individual rights or of aggregate benefits, we should start with discussion of ways of organizing production and distribution for meeting needs in a way that be non-destructive of capabilities or autonomous agency; h) this implies avoiding transformation of global justice into a utilitarian program of global beneficence that may be led to give priority to intense desires vis-à-vis urgent needs; i) this implies also giving a critical basis to current economic categories; see for example the very idea of 'aid' that carries the Gricean 'implicature' of its being – unlike progressive taxation within one national society – a transfer not requested by justice; l) and a world organized on the basis of Kantian justice would not be a world of political and social uniformity, since several different ways of social organization would meet the requirements of justice, for fundamental principles are not *universal* but instead *universalizable*.

The deservedly famous work by Amartya Sen happened to cross such developments in ethical discussion coming from an opposite starting-point, namely discussion on the foundations of economic theory. Sen is known firstly for having proposed an alternative, centered on the 'capabilities approach' to interpersonal comparison of utility, which was one of the sore points of neo-classical economic theory. His proposal was measuring not satisfaction of preferences but instead well-being, a magnitude distinguished – as Arthur C. Pigou had suggested – from strictly economic 'welfare,' and which indicates one's quality of life, that may be understood as a set of "functionings" in turn consisting either of "states" (as being in good health, or being adequately fed) or "activities" (as having self-respect) and constitutive of one person's being.[46] In turn the capability of functioning consists of various combinations of functionings that a person may acquire. Freedom, a notion that in political discussion was usually opposed to equality, should not be taken only as a means for acquiring something else, but should be included in well-being as one constitutive element since to be able to choose is an item of living and we should accordingly distinguish between doing x and choosing to do x and doing it. An assessment of well-being understood in these terms is quite different from utilitarian valuation of "states of affairs" in so far as it assigns to functionings and capabilities also a non-instrumental value. The utilitarian view of value as utility to which welfare economics has recourse acknowledges only individual utility and defines it in terms of a certain state of mind, pleasure, happiness, or satisfaction of preferences. Instead, being happy or satisfied cannot be considered to be the only important factor, unless other functionings be made meaningless or valued just as means.

The main result of Sen's capabilities approach is reinserting a number of dimensions that were traditionally classified as belonging to ethics into economic theory or the social sciences as a whole. The main idea is that if the social sciences are to deal with phenomena of under-development and poverty, or to account for historically given successful processes of growth/development they have to reintroduce such dimensions into the social sciences, not just qua subject-matter of some descriptive science but as a kind of evaluative or normative dimension that cannot be eliminated from a social science that be an empirical science, not a system of tautologies. In other words, the beginning of the twentieth-century facts-values dichotomy was so naïve and dogmatic that a truly empirical science cannot get rid of values, unless it ceases to be empirical.

A few comments on developments in development ethics may be the following:

a) there appear to be a few recurrent traits of the spontaneous emergence of a new sub-discipline, namely a relationship between social sciences and ethics that is neither dependence nor absorption, the fact of starting from some kind of widely acknowledged premises; the fact of carrying out the discussion not (pace MacIntyre) by juxtaposing competing claims and then raising one's voice louder and louder, but instead by modifying previous proposals through some kind of self-criticism guided by need to pay attention to the partner's good, or less good, reasons; O'Neill's proposal that assumptions be made as general as possible and that the content, not the foundation of the assumption, be the subject of agreement, spells out a typical unavoidable trait of applied ethics, that makes it something different from the still dogmatic top-down application of utilitarianism from Hare, Singer and others.

b) Again, O'Neill's proposal of keeping the distinction between justice and beneficence as tight as ever may help to avoid a surrender to relativism that both a utilitarian and a rights-based approach appear to carry in a highly paradoxical way, since both approaches are on principle objectivistic and universalistic; the trouble is that if you accept the concerned parties' definition of their own rights or their own utility you are caught into the nightmare of a night where all cows are black and all claims are equally warranted, maybe including third world women's claim to free genital mutilation provided by national health services; if, on the contrary one introduces a distinction by which duties of beneficence and duties to develop talents are selective, while justice is the first duty, but a duty concerning just the general social framework, and does not cover the whole of human existence, then the selective character of imperfect obligations is not offensive toward justice, granted that the former supplement justice and do not substitute it.

c) A third suggestion by O'Neill is that a kind of minimally Kantian ethics seems to be required by all partners in the discussion, in so far as argumentative procedures that may be accepted by different partners apart from their overall views need to turn around such *lato sensu* Kantian concepts as universalizability and procedural justice; this does not deny a role for utilitarian procedures in order to frame issues in a rationally arguable way once an agreement is reached on the character of the issues (a task about which utilitarianism has little to say), and recognized that the issue is one of allocation of resources and that the resource to be allocated is such as to admit of criteria of optimality; and on the other hand it lessens the role of a few notions from the Aristotelian tradition such as those employed by Amartya Sen's *capabilities approach*, once an agreement has been reached by autonomous subjects on the definition of the capabilities to be taken into account in the discussion (unless the approach become the Troy-horse of paternalism).

d) The astonishing discovery has been that ethics is not a luxury item to be consumed only in an affluent society, but instead it is good for poor countries; but a doubt may subsist about the qualification of such ethics; if poor countries need 'development' is it a development ethics that they need? Wouldn't liberation, justice, equality be more viable candidates than development? Doesn't the term hide a surplus of unnecessary connotation that comes unavoidably from the developed countries' self-image and doesn't it try to impose that image on different cultures? Perhaps some kind of negative determination (say, anti-hunger or anti-poverty ethics) could do better and would save applied philosophy from the danger of lapsing into preaching and edification; the same anti-idolatric preoccupation that Adorno sensibly manifested with the idea of socialism could help in adopting his suggested answer to the question:

what is the end to reach by bringing about a just and liberated society, to which he suggested that the only delicate answer would be

> the grossest: that no one should starve any more [...] In the ideal of the man free from inhibitions, creative, overwhelming with energy, precisely that fetishism of commodities has intruded itself that, in bourgeois society, carries inhibition and impotence.[47]

Applied Ethics is not Ethics *Applied*

In the various fields where the applied ethics revolution has taken place, what has made for the novelty of the phenomenon has been the circumstance that the new approach did not lie in applications of ready-made normative ethics to one given field. It is true that in the beginning of bioethics there were plenty of examples of this kind, first of all direct applications of utilitarian and neo-Thomist doctrines, and this is the feature which made bioethics look like the new candidate for the role of 'field of endless struggles,' but what happened at a rather early stage is that adepts to different, and indeed opposite philosophical schools – as Beauchamp and Childress were – found patterns of argument that were acceptable for both, their enduring dissent on more general issues notwithstanding. And in the last decades developments have been more innovative every time the discussion within the various branches of applied ethics has not followed closely the divisions of philosophical schools. The surprising novelty of the applied ethics phenomenon is related to the fact of being born inductively thanks to the joint effort of practitioners in several fields and philosophers, jurists, and theologians, of having followed the same path in different national contexts and in different domains, and finally, of having grown through a discussion between partners different not only in viewpoints and professional background but also in social roles, that is not only between practitioners of one field and specialists of various disciplines, but also between practitioners/specialists on the one hand and 'patients' (or 'stakeholders') on the other. That is, discussions in 'practical' ethics have been an unavoidable effect of the birth of movements aiming at participatory democracy. In all cases when the discussion of ethically sensible issues has become really participated and has involved movements and public opinions, the focus of concern has regularly shifted from familiar theoretical oppositions such as that between absolutism and relativism, or between consequentialism and deontology, or between the infamous sanctity and quality of life paradigms, but instead the ways of establishing what are the questions and who are the concerned partners who should have a say in the issue.

The lesson suggested may be that, instead of 'applied,' perhaps the adjective 'practical' would be more appropriate in order to connote the new genre in moral argument, or, in other words, ethics *qua* applied ethics is not a tool for convincing those who are already persuaded; it has a future and a possible function if understood in terms of a set of deliberative processes that may be enacted within the framework of an at least minimally liberal-democratic facing the fact of pluralism. Thus, applied ethics is not a 'container' where the right substantive contents may be stored; applied ethics is instead 'philosophically assisted deliberation' or a process of discussion among *distinct* and *dissenting* partners with different overall views and with diverging valuations of individual cases who negotiate solutions to real-world practical problems starting from their given set of beliefs and prescriptive principles and working out creative solutions, not minimal compromises, for cases of moral dissent.

The bet of applied ethics is that MacIntyre's description of the condition of moral pluralism in post-modern society is mistaken. MacIntyre described present-day societies as places where opposing partners advance arguments – say on the right to life vs. the right to choice, or on entitlements vs. distributive justice – that are simply "incommensurable," since they are based on criteria and standards not accepted by the opposing part. And yet such arguments claim to be rational and impartial arguments. This is why contemporary moral dissent has such a paradoxical air, and one may argue that such moral pluralism is not an orderly dialogue between different points of view, but instead "an unharmonious melange of ill-assorted fragments."[48] He concludes that – on the prevailing view of the nature of moral argument – we lack criteria with which we could convince our opponents and that apparently we are left to our own decision to adopt our own moral point of view. MacIntyre's diagnosis notwithstanding, I suggest that 'reasonable' solutions of moral debates, that is, solutions stronger than middle-of-the road compromises or decisions by majority rule since all the partners come out of the dispute having won something, can be achieved in various ways. This is possible because the solutions adopted are accepted, first, for reasons that are not always the same for the various partners of the discussion, and second, before reaching an overall agreement.

Applied Ethics is a 'Kantian' Approach for Non-Kantians

A *latu sensu* Kantian approach has been unavowedly adopted in discussions in applied ethics by all the parts without being previously converted to a comprehensive Kantian view in so far as a subject as self-ruler view and some criterion of universalizability are indispensable ingredients for any collective process of deliberation. Yet, procedures derived or inspired by opposite approaches are quite compatible with such an overall quasi-Kantian framework. Utilitarian ways of thinking are irreplaceable for approaching in some rational way a number of issues once the discussion procedures have reached a preliminary consensus about the nature of the issue (that is, once there is agreement about the idea that the problem is one of allocation of resources and that the agreed upon definition of the resource at stake is such that allows for a criterion of optimality, instead of a criterion of priority in need, or an equalitarian criterion, or free-market, as the basis for allocation.

For example a Kantian, or a follower of even more traditional kinds of moral theories such as Aristotelianism, Ciceronian natural law or Thomism, could have no objection to the adoption of QALYs for assessment of health policies. QALY, that is, Quality Adjusted Life

Year is a magnitude adopted as a measuring rod for comparing health policies.[49] Such a ways of assessing policies is clearly a Utilitarian way of thinking, but a utilitarian way of thinking is not declared to be wicked by any sensible followers of other theories; for the latter it is simply a criterion to be adopted in a well-defined number of cases, where, say, the virtue at issue is benevolence, not justice, and where it is a matter of positive, not negative duties; objections to adoption of the criterion may be raised on other grounds, for example: is the criterion 'ageist'? or: does it imply some other hidden bias?

Or, as another example, a few notions derived from the Aristotelian tradition, such as those implied by Amartya Sen's 'capabilities approach'[50] may have full citizenship when the discussion is about *what* is the subject-matter of rights, of just distribution, of equality, that is when the discussion makes room for the kind of considerations that were totally absent from Peter Singer's famous paper on famines and morality.[51]

Applied Ethics is Deliberation

After the controversy between the two mixed approaches in bioethics, that is principlism and casuistry, in the early eighties, and the attack on both by anti-theorists such as supporters of virtue ethics, of the care approach, of feminists ethics in the late eighties, a wave of Mild-Aristotelians, soft-Kantians, neo-Pragmatists have pointed at contextual knowledge, deliberation, radical democracy as the so-to-say 'method' for applied ethics. The conundrum has been aptly described by Winkler and Coombs as follows:

> Traditional moral philosophy has virtually identified the possibility of genuine moral knowledge with the possibility of universally valid ethical theory, and has supposed that all acceptable moral standards, of every time and place, can be rationally ordered and explained by reference to some set of fundamental principles. Perfect theoretical unity and systematisation may be impossible to obtain, because there may be a plurality of basic principles that resist ordering. But it is generally assumed that such principles will be

few in number, such that substantial and pervasive order may be discovered. A corollary to this conception of moral knowledge is the view that moral reasoning is essentially a matter of deductively applying basic principles to cases. However, contrary to expectations created by these methodological assumptions, many philosophers who ventured into clinics and boardrooms were chagrined to discover how little usefulness this deductive approach had in the confrontation with genuine moral problems [...] In the experience of many philosophers actually working in medical ethics, most of the real work of resolving moral problems occurred at the level of interpretation and comparison of cases. Recourse to abstract normative principles seemed never to override case-driven considered judgment. On the contrary, conflict between a putative principle and the extensive consideration of cases seemed always to result in refining the interpretation of whatever abstract principle was involved.[52]

The suspicion raised in the eighties and nineties against ethical theory by virtue theorists and anti-theorists was not against technicalities, but against the 'theoretical' character of normative systems such as utilitarianism and Kantian ethics.[53] What I will object is that Immanuel Kant's ethics was not 'ethical theory' in this sense,[54] and yet, the anti-theorists are even more right than they realize, since, after the proof of the co-extensional equivalence of act and rule utilitarianism, also a proof of the extensional equivalence of utilitarianism and Kantian ethics might be provided, based on the consideration that, taking *all* consequences over an *infinite* time-span into account, any decent utilitarian will conclude that promises should be kept, the truth told, and all traditional duties of the 'old morality' fulfilled, and that those who preach the 'new morality' are simply bad utilitarians; but this is not a real problem for the best among classical ethical theories, since the historically given Immanuel Kant – possibly to be distinguished from some of his followers – had clear in mind that ethical theory is a ladder you have to throw away once you have reached the top of the wall, where, while keeping your balance, you have to take real-world decisions, and here it is the faculty of judgment what really counts, since we easily reach an agreement on which rule to follow and we may keep discussing over the ages about the reasons why to follow it, but the real point, the point where decent persons are sorted out from villains, is not which rule to follow but instead which kind of situation are we facing, so that we may resort to the kind of rule to be applied to the given kind of situation. The big ethical question is: what is really going on around? For example, are we lying to the police as no good citizen should do (Italy, 1943) or are we hiding in a nunnery an innocent victim from unjust prosecutors? Or also, are we helping younger scholars from the right alignment (either 'Catholic' or 'Secular') as any good Catholic (alternatively: Secularist) has to (Italy, 2006), or are we *fixing* a competition for academic jobs that is supposed to be open to every candidate and run according to a set of rules? Once one agrees the kind of situation one is in is of the second kind in both instances, there is no need to remember whether one is a utilitarian or a Kantian, or a Thomist, to know that it is one's duty to do/not to do *b*.

The task of moral philosophy 'applied' to real-world deliberation might be described then as the task of clarifying over and over again our implicit ways of arguing in moral issues, and providing not the final solution, but more modestly, plural reasons for reaching the same practical conclusions either by discovery of lines of conduct that may be acceptable on the basis of different normative judgements, or by welcoming technical solutions that raise no objection by one side while silencing the moral objection that was raised by the other to previously proposed lines of action, or by finding virtuous compromises where everybody is content even if somebody has stronger reasons for appreciating the compromise.

The cumulative suggestion coming from the contextualist critics of ethical theories and the proponents of deliberative procedures seems to go in a roughly Aristotelian, or Pragmatist, or, as I suggest, 'Kantian' moral philosophy (once Kant has been read in the way the recent Kantian scholarship reads him), but this does not imply adhesion to any full-fledged version of Aristotelian or Pragmatist or Kantian philosophy. A good example of such suggestions is the way the Kantian philosopher

Onora O'Neill characterizes the way in which her own Kantian constructivism is concerned with real world processes of decision-making by subjects who have their own starting-points and world-views and may be enlightened by 'technicians of reason' not through brainwashing but instead through self-criticism. The function of the philosopher is to help in clarifying conceptualisation of issues, working out arguments from accepted premises, in self-enlightening the actors about their own comprehension of goals and values, not teaching the actors the right set of values or moral precepts.[55] The bet, in a word, is that you cannot be both rational and evil, that you can go wrong by yourself but can be right only together. This much, and not more, is the 'Kantian,' or Aristotelian or Pragmatist, element in any deliberation process.

Applied Ethics is Reverse Subversion

The emergence of applied ethics seems to contradict those prophets of calamity of the MacIntyre kind who deplore the loss of moral nerve by contemporary society, but also those merry post-moderns of the Richard Rorty kind who announce that all that was solid has now melted definitely into the air and no moral question is any more serious and such a lack of rigidity is the answer to moral issues. Indeed it seems to contradict those who in a first phase had apparently won most in terms of authority and circulation from the birth of applied ethics, that is the proponents of the Benthamite and Sidgwickian new morality. If one looks at developments that have de facto taken place in every area of applied ethics, Donagan's diagnosis of a "reverse subversion" may sound not out of place; that is, it is not only the most deed-seated assumptions of ordinary morality, probably coinciding with tradition and prejudice to be set at risk by use of rational argument on real-life issues as the proponents of the new morality believe, but also the pile of commonplaces that have sedimented in the shared opinions of educated middle class as a result of the teachings of the Utilitarians and the Emotivists in the Anglo-Saxon world and of the Historicists and the Existentialists on the Continent that tend to be eroded by public discussion on real-world issues. Developments in applied ethics have carried something quite different from any establishment of a 'new' morality as contrasted with a chimerical 'old morality'; indeed they have carried apparently a grand return of the most deprecated expressions of such old morality, casuistry and natural law thinking.

Casuistry, after the controversy between Pascal and the Jesuits, was unanimously detested without any further scrutiny by modern European philosophers, ranging from Adam Smith to Christian Thomasius and reaching Sidgwick.[56] A milder view was held by Kant, who believed that casuistry cannot be turned into a *technique* that may be presented in a handbook, but is bound to remain forever just an *art* to be learned through practice.[57]

In the last decades of the twentieth century, quite on the contrary, not only a "new casuistry" approach emerged in bioethics as one of the partners in the methodological competition in the assessment given by Albert Jonsen and Stephen Toulmin, according to which moral argument is made possible, even without sharing spelled out 'intermediate' principles as in Beauchamp and Childress's approach, by shared valuations of paradigmatic cases, but the whole of applied ethics shares with old casuistry a number of traits. The first is the idea that ethics is not only a 'protrepticon' to an ethical life, which is in itself a matter of 'art,' or of playing by ear, as it was for all the Rousseauvian and Romantic tradition, and still was for Nicolai Hartman, but is instead also a tool-box for reaching practical decisions shared by distinct and dissenting partners, practical decisions that are based on something more than unprincipled compromise or majority rule.

Natural law thinking was the bête noire of early twentieth-century philosophers (both neo-positivists and existentialists, besides epigones of Hegelianism such as Benedetto Croce). It was believed to be a residue of metaphysical cant. What is astonishing is that since the UN declaration of Human Rights the discussion about the issues of international order has been constantly construed in terms of a kind of new natural law thinking by virtually everybody, except a few hard-liners of act-utilitarianism and including those who still believed natural law to be pure nonsense.[58]

Applied Ethics is a Gift from Zeitgeist

In the western public sphere of the sixties there was apparently that kind of subversion of older values that so much scared some while making others believe that the end of superstition, prejudice, obscurantism had come for good. Movements in western countries such as counter-cultural movements, anti-Vietnam war movement, 'new movements' of any description (students, new kinds of workers' movements, women's liberation movements, gay liberation etc.) conveyed for a while the following message: let us overcome bourgeois moralism or hypocritical conventions (in the Latin countries it was always "*Catholic* moralism" for lack of direct experience of Protestant moralism), let's drop nonsensical talk of *values* in order to face *facts*, or the real world as it is. Campaigns for transformations of standard morality, particularly in matters of sexual mores, but also much rhetoric about revolutionary or 'liberationist' violence, and some themes in the early feminist campaigns for legalisation of abortion shared some of this immoralist bias; the shared element was the claim that discourse on real issues could only be carried out in value-free terms, that talk of just or unjust, or rights, or values was unavoidably ideological distortion of issues, or mental slavery from which the oppressed could only emancipate themselves by getting rid of internalised inhibitions.

In more sophisticated versions this was reflected in the revival of the young-Marx philosophy and the exposure of ideology as false consciousness and abstract morality as ideology. In an even more sophisticated version it was mirrored in the French Nietzsche-renaissance, where the discovery that all values were genealogically produced by something else – basically power – was felt to be a demystifying, and accordingly a leftist discovery.

In the eighties there was apparently a counter-trend or a fashion of value-laden discourse. Let me recall the enormous echo of the American bishops pastoral on economic justice, the echo of a few campaigns by Amnesty International and the growing diffusion of the language of "human rights."

This was mirrored at a more sophisticated level by the so-called "crisis of Marxism" in the countries where there had been a historically consolidated politico-social-intellectual Marxist block and by a comparatively quick popularity of Rawls's political philosophy or alternatively, but with less success, by Apel or Habermas's versions of discourse ethics. These seemed to promise an alternative ideology-political program to a-moral political ideologies and political programs such as historicist (Gramscian) or structuralist (Althusserian) Marxism or on the opposite front right-wing liberalism of the *Laissez Faire* kind. An incredible phenomenon of this kind was the wave of Rawlsianism that apparently galvanized the Italian Socialist Party led by Bettino Craxi in the eighties, shortly before its sudden disintegration as an effect of a wave of trials for bribery (the *Mani Pulite* affair) and the flight to Tunisia of the party's secretary!

Facing apparent anti-moralism of the sixties and apparent revival of political morality of the eighties one is tempted to ask whether *Zeitgeist* makes a U-turn every 20 years, or whether there are diverging trends in our culture. I venture to advance the conjecture that there are two long-run tendencies in our culture going in quite opposite directions, and that we are often caught in the middle.

The first is a 'nihilist' tendency to full 'autonomy,' and accordingly – among other things – complete demoralization of the various spheres of life, from science to law, politics, and the economy, so that these are ready to become a proper subject for technical governance. This is basically the diagnosis to be found in Theodor W. Adorno, Max Horkheimer, Hans-Georg Gadamer, Dietrich Bonhoeffer, and others. Obviously enough Martin Heidegger would fit into this assorted company if he were not the proponent of a kind of hyper-demoralization, fostering not a return to ethics but a run away from ethics, beyond technique into 'poiesis.' The tendency diagnosed by this group of thinkers is an ineluctable tendency, not a result of ill-will, as would suggest instead the most conservative and moralistic praisers of the old good times.

This nihilist tendency seems to be mirrored by existentialism, emotivism, theories of the death of ethics. When looked at from the viewpoint of the latter – let us think of Nietzsche's diagnosis of socialism and humanitarianism as still priest-like kinds of 'false' atheism – the nineteenth-century philosophies of history, anthropodicies, historicist or revolutionary political outlooks, and secular moralities seem to become some kind of intermediate steps, not completely secularised products of the process of secularisation.

The second and opposite tendency, which is perhaps too an inescapable tendency of our culture, not a product of human weakness, is the growth of what Arnold Gehlen named tele-ethics.[59] According to him, the world information system has blurred a number of moral dualisms which had always been deeply rooted in moralities (such as the duality between the moral code acceptable within the group and the one for external relations, between the morality of private individuals and the one for politicians; between the morality of the *pater familias* and the one for the *homo economicus*). Facing the overflow of information in the present-day world, the distinction between a moral code for in-group relationships and a moral code for relationships with strangers that anthropologists have detected in virtually every culture may hardly hold in present-day developed societies. A spontaneous tendency is applying received moral criteria on a wide scale and to domains previously immunized. This, according to Arnold Gehlen's conservative diagnosis, is a pathological attempt at bringing to life an unconceivable new moral faculty, namely a tele-ethics. Perhaps Gehlen is right to a point, and it is true that there is something pathological in campaigns trying to inculcate direct individual moral responsibilities and thus feeling of guilt for processes and events where cause-effect relationships are multiple, complex, and indirect, and where games are not zero-sum games since it can hardly be proved that a reduction in our per capita income could imply real and lasting benefit to starving third-world population, apart from immediate relief to victims of famines and epidemics. On the other hand, a number of issues raised in popular campaigns of the last decades years on issues such as peace, ecology or North-South economic relationships have been legitimately construed in terms of value-judgments and moral responsibilities, terms that were highly unpopular in the 'old' Left and taboo for right-wing liberalism of the nineteenth-century kind. It is true that such campaigns risked proving to be purely 'ideological' (in the Marxian sense) or unintended propaganda for one of the blocks at the time the world was split into two blocks; the present opposite risk may be that of going to an opposite extreme of anti-Machiavellianism and believing that everything depends on factors that are under our control and of which we are accordingly responsible.

In the heaven of academia, as contrasted with the terrestrial world of public discourse, there have also been tendencies and fashions, and sometimes they have mirrored or mimicked the tendencies and fashions of public discourse. And yet at least a few points are now somewhat less disputed than a few decades ago. They are the following:

a) claims of total subjectivity of moral valuations or, on the contrary, of the viability of a 'scientific' morality were popular at the beginning of the twentieth century and are now happily out of fashion;

b) the Benthamite 'new' morality, built from scratch on the basis of reason and empiricism, is left, happily enough, only in the agenda of a tiny sect of Utilitarians;

c) the boundaries between more Kantian and more Aristotelian currents in ethics have become less and less waterproof, and the discovery of several methods of applied ethics illustrated in this chapter has made the discussion of public issues in moral terms possible here and now, without waiting for complete erasure of such boundaries;

d) what we are left with is perhaps something less than a full-fledged 'rehabilitation' of normative ethics; perhaps we are left with "normativity within the bounds of plural reasons," but I dare to say that this is one of the cases where *less* is in fact *more*.

This is possibly a stubbornly optimistic way of looking at the world. As Giovanni De Grandis commented in his review of my book on twentieth-century ethics, perhaps my own view of contemporary discussion in ethics as a discussion around a round table where 'reasonable' arguments are finally advanced and criticised, after the hard times of the first half of the twentieth century where either historicist or linguistic shears were employed on both sides of the Channel in order to cut normative ethics into pieces, is biased: perhaps

> the problem is that Cremaschi is committed to bringing us good news about ethics, its usefulness and robustness. Such hidden optimism vitiates against the narrative because it risks either eliminating or curtailing with a *cordon sanitaire* the unwelcome guests at the ethical symposium: nihilists, sceptics, relativists, stubborn post-modernists, anti-theorists, deep pessimists etc. ... The most disquieting feature of the metaphor of the dinner table is that it is something more than a metaphor: it captures the weight and the impact that ethical discourse has on the contemporary world: more or less that of dinner table chats.[60]

A Provisional Moral

What I have developed in the present essay is neither a theoretical nor a historical argument. I have tried to spell out the meta-narrative of my reconstruction of the history of twentieth-century ethics. I cannot dare to enounce strong theoretical conclusions, since such conclusions require being backed by a theoretical argument. My claims are more lessons to be drawn from a story, perhaps a story that I have told in one particular way precisely because of the lessons I expected to draw, even if I was not aware of the denouement before working out the plot. Perhaps knowing is remembering and I had a happy end ready to be told without being aware of it. Nonetheless, as happens in the best circles, circularity is not necessarily vicious, and precisely because the bigger a circle, the less prone it is to vice. So, let me spell out a few tentative, modest, and provisional lessons:

1. deprecated casuistry is more alive than ever;
2. nasty natural law thinking is still the framework within which we are bound to formulate public issues;
3. moral dilemmas never arise; life is full of tragic conflicts, but they are between duty and luck, never between two duties;
4. moral dissent is not a (deprecated or exalted) mark of the modern secular world; it cannot be settled either by the triumph of the new secular morality or by a grand return to the good old objective values, but it is treatable, or it may be at least restricted, by the right strategy;
5. practical philosophy cannot reach the same degree of exactness as the purely theoretical sciences, but in a sense different from the Aristotelian, that is, deliberation in real life consists less of top-down derivation of particular rules from general principles than in interpretation of contexts.

In other words, the point about which the anti-theory movement was right, and Bentham, Sidgwick and Singer desperately wrong, is that you will never be able to 'apply' an ethical theory to decision-making. When you come to deliberation, you will never have at hand but also (happily enough) never need a sort of case book of morals like a guide to etiquette.[61]

NOTES

[1] Brenda Almond, "Applied Ethics" in *Routledge Encyclopedia of Philosophy*, ed. by Edward Craig, 10 vols. (London: Routledge, 1998), vol. I, 318–323, 318.

[2] Hugo A. Bedau, "Applied Ethics" in *Encyclopedia of Ethics*, vol. I, 80–84, 80.

[3] Elisabeth Anscombe, *Mr. Truman's Degree* [1956] in Ead., *Ethics, Religion and Politics* (Oxford: Backwell, 1981).

[4] Francisco de Vitoria, "De iure belli" in *Obras de Francisco de Vitoria: relecciones teologicas*, ed. by T. Urdanoz (Madrid: La editorial católica, 1960), pars secunda, art. 1.

[5] See John Rawls, *A Theory of Justice* (Cambridge, Mass: Harvard University Press, 1971); Van Raenseler Potter, *Bioethics. A Bridge to the Future* (Englewood Cliffs, NJ: Prentice-Hall, 1971); Richard Hare, *Applications of Moral Philosophy* (Oxford: Clarendon Press, 1972); Peter Singer, "Famine, Affluence, and Morality" *Philosophy and Public Affairs*, 1–3 (1972), 229–243.

[6] Albert R. Jonsen, *The Birth of Bioethics* (New York: Oxford University Press, 1998), x-xi.

[7] Edmund D. Pellegrino and David C. Thomasma, *A Philosophical Basis of Medical Practice: Toward a Philosophy and Ethic of the Healing Professions* (New York: Oxford University Press, 1981); Idd., *For the Patient's Good* (New York: Oxford University Press, 1988).

[8] See Robert M. Veatch, *The Patient-Physician Relation* (Bloomington, Ind: Indiana University Press, 1991).

[9] Tom L. Beauchamp and James F. Childress, *Principles of Biomedical Ethics* [1983] (New York: Oxford University Press, 2001).

[10] The National Commission for the Protection of Human Subjects of Biomedical and Behavioral Research, *The Belmont report. Ethical principles and Guidelines for the protection of Human Subjects of Research* (Washington D.C.: DHEW Publication No. (OS) 78-0012).

[11] Ibidem, 398.

[12] See Albert R. Jonsen and Stephen E. Toulmin, *The Abuse of Casuistry. A History of Moral Reasoning* (Berkeley: University of California Press, 1988).

[13] Ibidem, 257.

[14] Daniel Callahan, "Communitarian Bioethics: a pious Hope?" in *The Responsive Community*, vol. 6: 4 (1996), 26–33.

[15] Daniel Callahan, *The Troubled Dream of Life: Living with Mortality* (New York: Simon and Schuster, 1993).

[16] See Carol Gilligan, *In A Different Voice: Psychological Theory and Women's Development* (Cambridge, Mass: Harvard University Press, 1982); Nel Noddings (ed.), *Caring. A Feminine Approach to Ethics and Moral Education* (Berkeley, Ca: University of California Press, 1984); Sara Ruddick, *Maternal Thinking: Toward a Politics of Peace* (Boston, Mass: Beacon Press, 1989); Eve Browning Cole, Susan Coultrap-McQuin (eds.), *Explorations in Feminist Ethics: Theory and Practice* (Bloomington, Ind: Indiana University Press, 1992); Seyla Benhabib, *Situating the Self: Gender, Community, and Postmodernism in Contemporary Ethics* (New York: Routledge, 1992), 148–177; Mary

J. Larrabee (ed.), *An Ethics of care: Feminist and Interdisciplinary Perspectives* (London: Routledge, 1993); Virginia Held, *Feminist Morality: Transforming Culture, Society and Politics* (Chicago: Chicago University Press, 1993); Annette Baier, *Moral Prejudices* (Cambridge, Mass: Harvard University Press, 1994).

[17] See Onora O'Neill, *Faces of Hunger*, Ead., *Autonomy and Trust in Bioethics* (Cambridge: Cambridge University Press, 2002).

[18] Jonathan D. Moreno, *Deciding Together* (New York: Oxford University Press, 1995), 70.

[19] See John Rawls, *A Theory of Justice.*

[20] See Nelson Goodman, *Fact, Fiction, and Forecast* [1954] (Cambridge, Mass: Harvard University Press, 1983).

[21] Rawls, *A Theory of Justice*, 46-53.

[22] Ibidem, 51.

[23] Ibidem.

[24] Ibidem.

[25] Ibidem, 46.

[26] Ibidem.

[27] See Noam Chomsky, *Aspects of the Theory of Syntax* (Cambridge, Mass: MIT Press, 1965), 3–9.

[28] Ibidem, 58.

[29] Ibidem, 49.

[30] Ibidem, 53.

[31] Ibidem.

[32] W. David Ross, *The Right and the Good* [1930] (Oxford: Clarendon Press, 2002), 41.

[33] John Rawls, *Political Liberalism* (Cambridge, Mass: Harvard University Press, 1993).

[34] David A. Crocker, "Toward Development Ethics" in *World Development*, vol. 19: 5 (1991), 457–483, 457.

[35] Denis Goulet, *The Cruel Choice* (New York: Atheneum, 1977); Id., *Development Ethics: a Guide to Theory and Practice* (New York: Apex, 1995).

[36] Peter Berger, *Pyramids of Sacrifice: Political Ethics and Social Change* (New York: Basic Books, 1974).

[37] See Godfrey Gunatilleke, Neelan Tiruchelvam, Radhika Coomaraswamy (eds.), *Ethical Dilemmas of Development in Asia* (Lexington, MA: Lexington Books, 1983); Roberto Murillo, "Noción desarrollada del desarrollo" in *Revista de Filosofía de la Universidad de Costa Rica*, vol. 12: 35 (1974); Carlos Gutierrez, "Papel del filósofo en una nación en desarrollo" in *Revista de Filosofía de la Universidad de Costa Rica*, vol. 12: 35 (1974); Mario Bunge, *Ciencia y Desarrollo* (Buenos Aires: Ediciones Siglo Veinte, 1980).

[38] See http://www.development-ethics.org/

[39] See Denis Goulet, *A New discipline: Development Ethics*, Working paper # 231 (Notre Dame, Ind.: Notre Dame University, 1996).

[40] David A. Crocker, "Toward Development Ethics" in *World Development*, vol. 19: 5 (1991), 457–483, 457.

[41] Peter Singer, "Famine, Affluence, and Morality" in *Philosophy and Public Affairs*, vol. 1: 3 (1972), 229–243, reprint in *World Hunger and Moral Obligation*, ed. by William Aiken and Hugh La Follette, (Englewood Cliffs, NJ: Prentice-Hall, 1977), 22–36; see also Id., *Practical Ethics* (Cambridge: Cambridge University Press, 1979).

[42] Garrett Hardin, "Lifeboat Ethics: The Case against Helping the Poor" in *Psychology Today*, vol. 8, (1974), 123–126; reprint in Aiken and La Follette, *World Hunger and Moral Obligation*, 11–21.

[43] Garrett Hardin, "The Tragedy of the Commons" in *Science*, vol. 162 (1968), 1243–1248.

[44] Onora O'Neill, "Lifeboat Earth" in *Philosophy and Public Affairs*, vol. 4: 3 (1975), 273–292; reprint in Aiken and La Follette, *World Hunger and Moral Obligation*, 149–164, 154.

[45] Onora O'Neill, *Faces of Hunger. An Essay on Poverty, Justice and Development* (London. Allen & Unwin, 1986).

[46] Amartya Sen, *Inequality Reexamined* (Oxford: Oxford University Press, 1994), chs. 1 and 9.

[47] Theodor W. Adorno, *Minima Moralia. Reflexionen aus dem beschädigten Leben* [1951] in *Gesammelte Schriften*, 20 vols. (Frankfurt a. M.: Suhrkamp, 1972–80), vol. IV, 176.

[48] Alasdair McIntyre, *After Virtue* (Notre Dame, Ind: University of Notre Dame Press, 1981), 10.

[49] See John F. Kilner, "Healthcare resources, allocation of" in *Encyclopedia of Bioethics* ed. by Stephen G. Post (New York: MacMillan Reference USA, 2004), 1098–115.

[50] See Amartya Sen, *Resources, Values and Development* (Blackwell, Oxford, 1984) Id., *Inequality Reexamined* (Oxford: Oxford University Press, 1992).

[51] Peter Singer, "Famine, Affluence, and Morality" *Philosophy and Public Affairs*, vol. 1: 3 (1972), 229–243; reprint in Aiken and La Follette, *World Hunger and Moral Obligation*, 22–36.

[52] Earl R. Winkler and Jerrold R. Coombs, "Introduction" in Winkler and Coombs, *Applied Ethics: A Reader* (Oxford: Blackwell, 1993), 1–8, 2–3.

[53] See Stanley G. Clarke and Evans Simpson (ed.), *Anti-Theory in Ethics and Moral Conservatism* (Ithaca, NY: State University of New York Press, 1989).

[54] Immanuel Kant, *Über den Gemeinspruch: Das mag in der Theorie richtig sein, aber nicht für die Praxis* [1973] in *Kant's gesammelte Schriften*, ed. by the Berlin-Brandenburgischen Akademie der Wissenschaften (Berlin: Meiner and de Gruyter, 1902), vol. VIII, 273–313.

[55] See Onora O'Neill, *Faces of Hunger*.

[56] See Albert Jonsen, Stephen E. Toulmin, *The Abuse of Casuistry: A History of Moral Reasoning* (Berkeley, Ca: University of California Press, 1988).

[57] Immanuel Kant, *Metaphysik der Sitten* [1797] in *Kant's gesammelte Schriften*, vol. VI, 203–493, 411; Id., *Metaphysik der Sitten Vigilantius*, ibidem, vol. XXVII\2.1, 475–732, 701.

[58] Like, typically, the leading Italian political philosopher Norberto Bobbio in his *Giusnaturalismo e positivismo giuridico* (Milan: Edizioni di Comunità, 1965) where he formulated his own new legal positivism, and in his *L'età dei diritti* (Turin: Einaudi, 1992, Eng. transl. *The Age of Rights* (Cambridge: Polity Press, 1996); Swed. transl. *Rättigheternas epok* (Göteborg: Daidalos, 2000) where he articulates instead a rational universalistic justification of human rights.

[59] Arnold Gehlen, *Moral und Hypermoral* (Frankfurt a.M.: Athenäum Verlag, 1969), ch. 10.

[60] Giovanni De Grandis, "The Rise [and Fall?] of Normative Ethics. A Critical Notice of Sergio Cremaschi's *L'etica del Novecento*," 10.

[61] Iris Murdoch, *A Fairly Honourable Defeat* (London: Penguin 1970), 47.